# Psalms of a Sinner

# Psalms of a Sinner

by Eddie Doherty

with a Foreword by Catherine de Hueck Doherty

 ABBEY PRESS • St. Meinrad, IN 47577 • 1976

Abbey Press
St. Meinrad, IN 47577
©1976 by Madonna House

**Library of Congress Cataloging in Publication Data**

Doherty, Edward Joseph, 1890-1975.
    Psalms of a sinner.

    1. Meditations. I. Title.
BV4832.2.D63    1976     242'.4    76-226
ISBN 0-87029-058-4 pbk.

Printed in the United States of America

# Dedication

Our Lady of Combermere, all shining—in my fancy—and with three great stars blazing in your crown, to honor Father, Son, and Spouse, I offer you this book, as a child presents to his mother a necklace of crude beads he has fashioned, with her help, and strung together for love of her. You will turn them into splendor when your fingers touch them, and give them the look of Paradise. You are Paradise, for you hold God.

# Contents

*Foreward*

He was a celebrated reporter, but I didn't know it when he came into the storefront of our library in Harlem. He introduced himself as Eddie Doherty and then introduced the young woman who was with him. He bluntly stated that he came to see me because he had an assignment from *Liberty* magazine to write about the wickedest city in the world, namely, Harlem in New York City.

Yes, this was our introduction. The fact that I reacted violently to his statement about the wickedness of Harlem, and the fact that I asked him "Who made it wicked!" only seemed to arouse his interest more and more. He talked to me and left, but the very next day he returned to discuss Harlem, the Negro, the white man. But very soon he began discussing *me*.

Being a skilled reporter he soon found out a lot about me just by asking seemingly unrelated questions. As I came to know him I became interested in his background. I discovered that he was one of the most highly paid reporters in America at the time. He was a staff writer with *Liberty*, a script writer in Hollywood, a war correspondent in England, and later, editorial writer for the *Chicago Sun*. I also learned that he had a beautiful house in Westchester County, where taxes are high, that he owned a custom-made car and wore Donegal tweeds, that he knew everybody who was anybody, and a lot of nobodies who were really somebodies.

Yes, he was an interesting man. There came a day when he proposed to me, and even that proposal was different from any that I had ever heard about.

I had been worried about the burial of a poor Negro. We discussed it at length. Sometime in the afternoon he turned around and said to me, "How would you like to be buried with *my* people?"

Frankly, I didn't make the connection at all (not being Irish, I guess!) that this sentence was in fact a proposal. I thought he was still talking about the Negro I wanted to bury decently. It was only later, when we were in the subway on our way to Times Square, that I suddenly thought of that sentence. It dawned on me that the only people who are buried with one's people belonged to the family, and that factually he wanted me to belong to *his* family, and that was how he was proposing!

*X*    Well, after two years of saying no, there came a day when I said yes to his proposal. Still, I didn't see how we could be married. I was "wedded" to the Lay Apostolate of Friendship House which I had founded in Harlem in 1938, after having started the Apostolate itself in Canada some years previously.

Eddie was rich, and I had embraced total poverty. Eddie had a house, and I lived in a one-room apartment in Harlem. It just didn't add up. His final proposal was made to me before Bishop Sheil of Chicago. The Bishop told him that I couldn't leave Friendship House, that he would have to join it; and that would mean giving up his job and his house, and distributing his money.

Eddie agreed. We were married by the Bishop on June 25, 1943. We lived in a small, ramshackle apartment after we were married. When the opportunity arose to start work in Combermere, Ontario at the invitation of the local Bishop, thus entering the rural apostolate, Eddie, without hesitation, came with me. Grace Flewelling, a staff worker, also came with us. We called this new apostolate "Madonna House."

Eddie died on the fourth of May, 1975. On the twenty-fifth of June, 1975, we would have been married thirty-two years.

Strange, this man who proposed to me by inviting me "to be buried with his people" was buried "with our people." He is buried in a little cemetery in Combermere, Ontario, Canada, next to a little white church not far from Madonna House. He is surrounded by some of our staff who died and whom he always liked to call "our children."

Somewhere along the line Eddie and I had taken vows of poverty, chastity and obedience. That was some twenty-two years ago. Perhaps, out of this chastity, our "children" were born—eighty-five women, twenty-six laymen and fourteen priests.

Before he died he wanted so much to finish *Psalms of a Sinner*. He did finish them. You are about to read them now. Perhaps I am prejudiced—I could be—but somehow to me they are the "psalms of a saint" (with a small *s*, that is).

*Catherine de Hueck Doherty*

Psalm 1

*The fool has said in his heart, "There is no God."*  3

But, Lord, he was strapped in tightly by the seat belt of his own ignorance to save him from any collision with wisdom or with truth!

I am a fool too: and a sinner. But I know You are, You were, You always will be. And I send You thanks for letting me see the splendor and the glory of Your creation.

The other fool should have been with me that beautiful May day some years ago when You let me see the miracle of the fish.

That fool, in the belief that he is an intellectual, asks the believers, "Which came first, the chicken or the egg?"

He thinks this will confuse Your children and convert them to anarchy and atheism and despair.

Any fool knows that an egg of itself can produce nothing. No life will ever scratch its way out of its sterile walls. If it is cracked, it emits only a noxious odor.

Any fool knows that it takes a rooster and a hen to produce an egg that will give life; and that both must be created before there can be an egg.

It is like asking, "Which came first, the woman or the womb?"

Three fish came swimming toward me that lovely morning. Rather, they were drifting toward me just under the surface of the stream. One was a big fish, that is, he was six or seven inches long. A speckled trout as masculine as a stallion or a bull. I had only to look at him to know that You had made him to be the master of his school.

Two females kept formation a little in front and to the right and left of the big fish. I knew they were feminine because they were in such beautiful contrast to the male.

They came close, very close. The big fish shuddered through his whole body. Little waves of sperm shot from beneath him to bless the sides and bellies of the female fish and the areas about their tails, and fertilize the hundreds or thousands of tiny eggs they held.

God's way with fish!

I could have said to the fool, the other fool, "Which came first, the trout roe or the trout?"

That day You also let me see two snails courting in

4 the shelter of a rock and a pair of dragonflies locked in love on the top of the rock, their blue-enamelled bodies making a beautiful oval.

How sensibly and simply You carved those snails. Did You tailor their houses to their measure? How exquisitely You made the dragonflies.

Male and female created He them.

And You said to them, "Increase and multiply." Only You could give such a command. Only You could give to each of Your creatures such a love of life; and a life of such love.

Fish and snails and insects and all of us are in Your care; but more than half the people in the world do not care for You, God, do not even know You.

I am a fool, Lord, and I am a sinner, so it is right for me to sing Your praises. Only a sinner can praise You on earth. Only a saint can praise you in heaven. One has to be a saint to enter heaven. But a sinner can be a saint if he asks for help. Some sinners do and some don't.

I give You thanks especially because I was, and am, so dastardly. Were I not, Your almighty strength might never have come to me. Your mercy might never have visited me.

I was like one of Your lost sheep.

Nay, I was not lost nor strayed.

I was a rebel and I fled Your flock in furious anger, and in a most unholy hatred, and in the firm resolve that never, never, never, would I return to You—never, never, would I bow my head at the mention of Your Name.

Had I not been a wicked lamb, Your Son, My Lord, My Shepherd, would not have hunted for me.

I would never have known the joy of being carried in His arms the long, long way back home.

I would not have held my foolish head against His breast.

I would not have heard the heartbeat of His infinite compassion. Nor would I have heard the melody sung Him by all Your galaxies of worlds and constellations —Your choirs of millions of billions of stars—Your marching bands of planets, each faithful to the intricate orbit You made for it, all praising You in eternal perfect harmony and order.

Had I not been a sinner, Lord, Your Son would never have written before me on the sands.

He stooped and wrote with His finger.

No man knows what He wrote; no man, but me.

He wrote down all my sins and He bent over so that I might not see myself as He saw me.

I did not look up, but I saw His breath blowing the sands away, even as He wrote.

And I knew that I had been forgiven and would no longer feel the heaviness of guilt.

My sins were blown away!

They have been blown away again and again, always by the compassion of Your Son's sweet-smelling breath.

But sometimes, Lord, some small grains of sand sting and wet my eyes; and it is then, only then, I think, that I realize I love You.

And I know I must cling to You or go blind.

Had I not been so wretched and ragged a sinner, I might never have known the tenderness and the love and the thoughtfulness and the care and the holiness of My Father.

I did not rise from the pigsty of my life and go to seek You, Lord; You came all the way to my filthy place.

You washed me clean.

You placed fine robes upon my nakedness.

You put a ring upon my finger.

You killed the fatted calf for me and, lo, I have been feasting at Your table all these many years!

You made a great room for me in Your heart, and a little niche (for Yourself) in my heart.

You put Your own furniture in that niche, and You sit there constantly playing hymns to me on Your golden harp.

Lord, sometimes I ignore You.

Sometimes I do not hear the music Your divine fingers make as they pluck the strings of Your harp.

Sometimes I am deaf even to Your singing voice.

But You do not forget me ever—even for a moment.

I am a sinner and You sing me psalms!

Why should I not sing my psalms to You?

*The girl was young and very pretty but she was not happy.*

She was dressed all in black. Over her charcoal hair she wore a charcoal snood but the thunderhead mood she wore was blacker than anything else.

"Help me," she said. "Tell me God is good. Tell me He wants me to be happy. The days when I was a nun have come back to me. The most horrible days of my life! For God's sake, help me!"

"What's horrible about being a nun?" I asked.

"It's this business about mortifying the eyes. It was the mistress of novices. 'If you see a tree and you see it's beautiful, don't look at it,' she said. 'If you see a flower, pretend not to. If you hear a bird singing, do not look and do not listen. If you look up at the stars at night, shut your eyes quickly.' Poor thing, I don't think she was ever happy.

"I couldn't stand the life. The other nuns stayed in the convent; I had to go or kill myself."

I kissed the tears from her eyes, told her to open them wide and look at everything around her. I left her and went my way up the steep sandy hill, rejoicing at the sun and the wind, the smell of pine trees, and talking to You.

Don't look at the stars!

David, the great-great-grandfather of Our Lord, sang sweetly of the stars. "When I behold Your heavens, the work of Your fingers, the moon and the stars which You set in place . . ."

Some lines of Longfellow came: "Silently one by one in the infinite meadows of heaven blossomed the lovely stars, forget-me-nots of the angels."

I thought of the Wise Men who followed a star and I remembered Abraham whom You love so much.

My friend, Ben Aronin, talks about Abraham in his epic poem, *The Abramiad:*

Behold, from the roof . . .
I sent my glance to the heights of heaven,
And I saw the hosts of the
    height . . . the stars of Yah!
This one after this one going,
To show to the sons of man
Times, seasons and festivals . . .

And Sin Nannar among them.

Sin Nannar was a temple of the moon. The moon was a god in the land of Ur and Abraham's father was the priest of the moon.

And even he . . his path was set,
Not to turn aside from it,
To the right or left.
Let not the anger of my father be kindled,
And I will speak this once.
For how can I quench my anguish?
Words like coals of fire
Burn my heart.
They are not master . . . they, the stars . . .
But slaves! . . .
As slaves walk quietly
Before their master,
Thus do they walk
In their pathways.
Therefore, no more will I give prayer to Sin,
But to the Master of the world . . . to Yah! . . .
Possessor of heaven and earth . . .
God the Most High . . . Awesome God!
Was . . . Is . . . and Will Be!
Father of all . . . Master of all . . . The All!
One! . . .

Lord, how can anyone learn to love You who is not allowed to look at You?

I picked up a dandelion as I travelled up the hill. It had bleached its hair. I blew on it, loosing a storm of tiny stars into the sunlight, each the seed of a gold and green dominion. And I remembered a moon I saw in Arizona.

Jack Scanlon and I were motoring across a wide mesa in the high mountains. We were on top of Your world. The sun was sliding slowly down the western sky, and You were tinting the white and gray clouds crimson and purple and gold.

The moon was high in the east. A full moon. The ghost of a moon. The blown dandelion of a moon. If a man could get close enough to it, he could blow it into a million spindrift stars.

The sun slipped out of sight and we watched You mix

the colors to mark its exit. You smudged the bright hues with the charcoal You use for night effects. You hovered over the spot like a mother who has just put her child to sleep, and You set the sentinel stars.

I loved You intensely then, like a lonely child who has suddenly found his father. There have been few such moments in my life. Today that intense love came back.

A woodpecker high up on a telephone pole was telegraphing You.

"Love, love, love."

I managed to translate his code. "Love, love, love, love, love, love." Then, of course, there was the last word, "love."

A small butterfly lay in the sandy loam. It had been downed by last night's storm. Its blue wings still had a sheen but not the magic powder that comes off on a fellow's fingers. Its blue was more glorious than the dragonfly's, or the sky's. It was almost as lovely a color as my Catherine's eyes.

Another bird claimed my attention. His breast was as yellow as the dandelion in the spring, or the goldenrod in the fall. St. Elizabeth's apron, full of yellow roses, could not have been so exciting. It lighted up my day.

The wild roses were enjoying a circus rehearsal. Pink costumed acrobats were climbing up and down their vines, leaping from branch to branch, rolling on the shiny wet grass, high wire walking, dancing, clowning. A few lifted their faces to You in fragrant song. What little rain was left on them shone like royal lace.

I filled myself with their aroma, as, I hope, You fill Yourself with the perfume of our prayers.

Great black and yellow bumblebees wooed the roses. By proxy and by pollen. They had just come from some bachelor roses in the woods. They were not interested in romance. They were interested in trade. It was business as usual with the bees. Pollen for honey. Traders first. Matchmakers second.

A silken flight of black and yellow butterflies, Your children of light, skimmed gaily over bees and roses. Two combinations of gold and ebony! An exquisite contrast to the jumble of pink and green! A golden mosaic!

A long thin rope of ink rippled and wriggled across the

road. Striped ink! Black and green and gold. A garter
snake. Lord, who gave it that name, and why? Shall we
see it advertised someday—"Live elastic, in fetching
stripes, for every woman of fashion?"

I looked down a sloping hillside and saw daubs and
dabs and dots and dashes of waving colors.

Red and white and purple clover. Lacquered buttercups. Pale yellow spears of mullein. Threads of purple
vetch. Clusters of creamy yarrow lace. Poppies and
thistles that mimicked glowing coals. Flickers of the
devil's paintbrush burning everywhere like the lighted
ends of cigarettes in a darkened room. Red and yellow
columbines. Touches of wild iris.

And milkweed flowers hanging from green stalks, in
neat bunches of long-stemmed pinkish-lavender stars,
getting ready to be wrapped in stiff brown pods and
pressed into gossamer astronauts by September. Masses
of tall grasses, timothy, and daisies.

Beauty on the stem! Hay on the hoof! Hay bowing and
prostrating itself before You. Hay rolling joyously down
to the dark blue ribbon of the river. Hay, clean and
scented as a woman's hair. Hay in June, waiting for the
reaper and the barns.

Some beauty leaps. Some beauty flies. Some beauty
creeps. Some beauty lives in Your winds. Some beauty
sings in the mind. All beauty sings of You.

A grove of poplars stopped me. Quaking, shaking,
shivering, quivering, shimmering, whispering, rustling,
gossiping, giggling, restless trees.

They greeted me with continuous salaams. I watched
the play of the leaves. Dark green or light green, depend-
ing on the movement of sunshine or shade. Like stained
glass windows, except that it had life.

A green frog jumped into the yellow rivulet alongside
the road, to avoid the hunting serpent.

A crazy butterfly with big red polka-dotted sails zig-
zagged low above the stream, pretending it was a convoy
pursued by enemy submarines. His wings flashed me a
message: "God loves you."

I sat down for a moment on Your crazy quilt of splendor. I remembered how once I had bitterly hated You.
You stole into my unwilling and rebellious heart through

my eyes, through my ears, through the nostrils of my nose, through my touch, through my thoughts.

You sang in my blood without my awareness. You took possession of me until my pulse caught the cadence of Your Son's Name, and beat to it every second—Jesus, Jesus, Jesus, Jesus.

All I have to give You, Lord, is me. All I have and all I am.

Hay on the hoof! That's me! I'm Your hayfield! Reap me when You're ready and I'm ripe.

How simple it would be if I were a spider! Then I would spin You a web of the finest silk, out of my body. I would hang it where You could see it the first thing in the morning.

Your dew on every delicate thread! And Your sun's rays hitting it just so!

But I can spin You only a web of words. "Lord, have mercy on me a sinner."

The girl in black was picking long-stemmed violets from the little rill that flows down the road. She looked up as I came down the hill.

She smiled at me. And I saw that You too had kissed her tears away.

Psalm 3

*I am no longer the colt of an ass, O Maker of mules and*
*men.* I am full-grown and bending with the years, but I can still carry You and Your Son into Jerusalem, to the cheering Hebrew children.

The Lord rests easily upon my back. I feel no weight at all. Rather, I feel young and free and joyful.

The crowds have gone. The road is silent and empty and, as He predicted, the very stones cry out. The road runs upward from a curve as tender and mysterious as a young girl's arm.

It is patched with small wooden bridges to hide the brook that laces it from top to bottom like a soft blue sash.

There is nothing but dust and stones today, but the stones cry out the glory of the Lord.

All the way up and down this road they flash their smiles at You and shout Hosannas. The branches and the trees shout with them. Not palm trees, Lord, but oaks and elms and maples and sometimes a poplar or a birch.

The stones are little bits of feldspar. They have a lacquer, a sheen, a joyful polish. They are in all exultant colors—reds, purples, wine, yellows, voluptuous blues.

They are many shapes. They vary in size from a pinhead to a kernel of ripe corn, or a boy's first yanked-out tooth. They vie with rubies and emeralds and amethysts and sapphires and opals.

It is not only the stones that cry out to You this glorious day.

The new flounce on the cedar's apron. The new guimpe on the petticoat of the towering pine. The little green orchestra of the fiddlehead ferns. Even the feathers of an oriole and of an owl proclaim Your glory and give You thanks and praise. And the moss—so many different kinds of moss—makes itself a royal carpet for Your donkey's feet.

It was a cloudy morning. It had rained in the night and there had been a slight sprinkle during breakfast, but as we started up the road the sun strode away with a group of clouds, who were trying to get its autograph. It looked upon the little stones, and lo, I was riding up a milky way of daystars!

Thanks, My Lord, for taking me away from the big

cities and putting me here. Thanks for showing me the miracles of Your creation.

Thanks for showing me today the real virtues of the brook that crisscrosses the road so many times.

Yesterday it was just water going somewhere in a hurry singing a silly song. Today it is a shepherd driving its flocks of pebbles and twigs and falling leaves down to the shining river, singing pastorales.

It is a landscape gardener changing the look of the country as he pleases and hiding old bottles and old cans.

Thanks for showing me that novice birch as she struggled out of her tight-fitting, waxy, bronze uniform into the informal, cool, white and pink habit of her order. She will be a birch forever.

Thanks for showing me millions of buds on the trees all around me. They were like so many impish newsboys, I thought, waiting for the five-star final. Each was poised on his branch, ready to race down the road and shout the headlines.

Thanks for turning me around so that I could look down and see the blue-gray of the river. It fitted in with the bewildering greens of the bushes and trees and mosses and ferns, the twilight gloom of the sandy road and the white-gray-black scatter rug of clouds.

Lord, You blend colors skillfully.

I paused a moment listening not to You but to a wood-pecker, machine-gunning his way into the pantry of a ghostly pine. I listened to the screeching of the blue jays. The birds flew away and all was still again.

I turned to take You back down the hill. The brook was still singing, "Alleluia, Alleluia, Alleluia." The little stones lay in a shadow, silent as the dusk.

Dead leaves were rotting at the side of the road. New trees were growing. New bushes were stirring into leaf.

Death and birth danced cheek-to-cheek all around us.

Palm Sunday was over, and good Friday lay ahead.

*Psalm 4*

*Lord God, our Destination, our Joyful Trysting Place, where all roads end, where all roads come together, You showed me something wonderful today.*

When I was a child my father used to sing me to sleep, sometimes, with a song about daisies: "Daisies Won't Tell." This morning You let me know that daisies will tell me many secrets if I listen. They were strung along the path on both sides of the road and they reminded me, somehow, of the lampposts that used to border the streets of Chicago. Maybe it was the way they were spaced; maybe it was something else.

The lamplighter came each evening just about dusk. He carried a lot of equipment including a ladder.

He placed the ladder carefully against the post, climbed slowly and squirted a blue flame into the lamp.

In a moment or two the lamp would burst into brilliant light—a miracle for me.

"But," one of the daisies whispered, "God doesn't go to all that trouble. When He wants to light your path He simply says, 'Let there be daisies,' and immediately we are at your ankles."

Angels or daisies, we are all His messengers. We obey His commands with joy.

Lord, You have been hemming my paths with daisies ever since I was born.

Even when I wandered far away from You, far from any thought of You, there were daisies all around me.

Janice Davis, in her whimsical poem, "The Good Child's Flower-Bed of Beasts," classifies roses as "jealous beasts," pansies as "humble beasts," and violets as "timid beasts."

But she didn't find anything beastly about the daisies.

I think I like the daisy best,
It laughs and nods and dances
It seeks the meadow and the ditch,
As vagabond as Francis.
And like that joyful little man,
The merry clan of daisies
Lift ragged arms and shining eyes
To sing their Maker's praises.

I bent down to pick one of the flowers.

"We're lighting not only your path," it said, "but all

God's bounteous table. Let your flat, pigeon-toed feet go
slowly up and down the road, and let your eyes be even
more gluttonous than they are now.

"See slowly. You can't see everything at once. You
can't gulp God's wonders in one swallow.

"Eat with appetite and don't make a hash of it nor a
salad. Eat with your ears also, and with your nose. The
smell of pines is for dessert."

In the light of the daisies, I saw that You had ripened
the raspberries for me. You had waited in ambush in the
sweet raspberry jam bush. Raspberries at my elbows.

Strawberries at my feet. Blackberries in the woods
ahead of me. And mushrooms waiting in the woods!

A red bird flew across the road and vanished into a
green whirlpool of aspen leaves. It was a crimson flame,
Lord, more exciting and more miraculous than the blue
flame of the old lamplighter. I called it the lamplighter
bird.

Quite a distance ahead of me I saw something that
looked like a mahogany four-poster bed. It was rocking
as though a great wind were shaking it. When I came
closer I saw it was a horse. A rocking-horse. Yet, not a
rocking-horse at all.

He was rolling in the dust, his legs up, kicking with
joy. Perhaps a horse's way of giving You thanks and
praise.

A black squirrel watched the horse for a time then
went to investigate the rumor that hazel nuts were soon
coming home again.

A gray rabbit sat in the dust and looked at me for a
long while. When he was sure I was not a carrot he
vanished into the bush.

A green and yellow leaf came scampering across the
dirt—the child of aging Summer and adolescent Autumn.

It was too pretty to let lie there. I picked it up and
thrust it into my basket of stones.

Butterflies kept flying around me as though I were
some freak that they might study; or as though they were
gaudy angels wondering what on earth You see in men,
especially sinners like me, that You should love them so.

The sky looked down with the serene blue-wonder of a
child.

The dusk was thick and I remembered my friend Father Brière. On the eve of his Silver Jubilee he said a prayer, "Lord, if You wish to give me a present, give me a little rain."

He didn't want it for himself, of course, he wanted it for the farmers who needed it so badly. When he woke next morning it was raining, and he gave You a Mass of thanks.

The dust was so thick on the stones that I had to wash them in the creek to see if they were worth carrying home. Some were good, some indifferent. I laved them and saved them. Or I laved them and left them.

I am glad You do not deal with sinners as I do with stones.

You love us all, even the ugly and the useless stones. You want to take all of us home.

What, Lord, has become of the old-fashioned girl who used to ask the daisies to tell her fortune? The daisies talked if she pulled their petals and counted them as they fell.

"He loves me. He loves me not."

The daisies loved to tease the little girl. It was only in their last petals that they told her the truth: that the man was a cad, a scoundrel, a false-hearted ghoul and he had a wife in every city, or that he was a gentleman and a hero and a scholar and a tender lover.

The girl was always glad, glad, glad, glad. She had found him out in time. She knew now he had never loved her at all, not even a smidge. Wasn't she the luckiest girl in the world? Or he really loved her. Wasn't she the luckiest girl in the world?

Who can imagine the modern girl taking her problems to a daisy instead of to a computer or a psychoanalyst?

I ate Your banquet with my eyes and ears and nose. I gorged on it, but I also had time to exult in Your gifts of taste and touch.

Through Your fields, wide and narrow, I went picking yarrow.

I visited our herb garden and sniffed a piece of heliotrope given me by the girl who tends the garden. A girl who looks as much like a daisy as a daisy looks like a girl.

Lord, I am only a thick-skinned thistle, rooted in the ditch that runs through the dance hall of the daisies. I am content to remain a thistle so long as You give me the sun of Your love and the abundant rain of Your mercy.

You love daisies. You love sparrows.
I imagine You can love thistles too.
I know You love sinners best of all.
That's what I learned today.

Psalm 5

*It is written, Lord, that a day in Your courts is better than a thousand years spent elsewhere; and that a thousand years in Your sight are like a day, a day awakened from its sleep.*

Today the little satchel of my heart is crammed almost to bursting with the glory all around me in this court of Yours on earth.

This is a perfect October day and I offer it to You with all my love, to be stretched into a thousand years of praise and adoration, a million years, an eternity of years, ever since the first moment when Your divine mind thought of me and decided to give me life.

I go slowly along roads that run through tall banks of painted trees. I go up to a painted hilltop. I go down to a painted valley. There is a painted sky above and a painted stretch of water far away and far below.

The air is full of glistening gossamer, living seeds born of dead milkweeds and dying thistles.

Here comes a milkweed seed dancing like a snowflake. It looks like a snowflake with long false eyelashes. It kisses a flaming maple leaf and skitters on and up and out of sight.

The valley is a magnificent burning bush, much greater than the one that frightened Moses.

I love October, hence I give it to You, Lord.

It is for me a prayer book with millions of pressed flowers and holy pictures and fourleaf clovers between its leaves.

It is a library of golden memories.

The sun has a special light this day, a soft light, an eerie light, a light that accents all the colors in the woods and sharpens every detail of Your creation; the enchanted and enchanting light that comes only in October.

The world around me lifts itself to You today, thanking You for its loveliness, glorifying You, adoring You, offering itself like an amorous woman—even as I do—and singing to You with many-scented winds. Listen to it, Lord:

"Living Lord of the living and the dead, can Your heaven be half so beautiful as Your earth?"

The world stands on its tiptoes, lifting itself to the height of the trees, to the tops of the highest ridges, and up to the string of clouds that have just come up into Your sky like sheep from the shearing.

The trees lift their arms with colored treasure—acres and acres and acres of waving, swaying, dancing, marigold-yellows and tulip-reds and strange and exotic orange and pink and brown and purple and green leaves.

Your leaves are pale green in the spring, Lord, not green in the fall. What would we do without Your million shades of green?

I listened a long time to the trees as they inquired about Your heaven and I listened to Your voice as You answered:

"My heaven? Come up and see."

Leaves were falling all around me like glowing sparks, like burning embers from a tremendous conflagration. Leaves were making a carpet of many colors for my clumsy feet.

I picked one up. It was a delicious scarlet, except for the crest You painted just above the stem, and that was yellow-gold.

I picked another and another from rustling piles around my ankles and noted that each was perfect.

And I knew by that magic light of Your sun that each of the billions of leaves on the thousands and thousands of trees on the hills around me was added proof of Your protection and Your love.

Yours is a divinely crazy love, infinitely mad and overwhelming love.

And we give You so little in return!

Dear God, please put my name on each of those leaves, on each of those adoring trees. My name and the names of all those I love, the living and the dead. All those who write to me and ask my prayers, all those in trouble, all those who need You most, especially those who do not know You love them, nor dream how divinely You love even the least of them.

Out of the leaves I picked an acorn, a pine cone, and a tiny winged seedpod.

Leaves of death and corruption, seeds of resurrection and of immortality.

And things come up to You, Lord.

They do not fly up like the birds.

They come up to You by falling to the earth and into the earth. They are of the earth. They must come up to You through the earth.

I shall come up to You too through the earth.

Shall I find heaven half so beautiful as the earth, if indeed I find it?

I heard Your voice speaking of a land of milk and honey, speaking of a ground that is holy, speaking of life and death in soothing whispers:

"Death is natural. Death is kind. Death is holy. Death is essential to the continuance of life upon this earth.

Look around you and see that this is true.

Death is splendor.

Death is born of life and life is born of death."

The winds stopped singing as I ventured back down the road and I heard the blue jays in the groves.

Even in a world like this, Lord, there must be screeching blue jays and mocking crows.

But leave them in this October day which I present to You, for I know You love them too and that You care for them as tenderly as You care for all Your other creatures.

_Source of all beauty and all truth, a few days ago You served me an egg; and I have not yet fully digested all the wonder of it._

I was walking up the road when You showed it to me.

The sun was unusually bright and I could see clearly all the stones, however little, that had been washed into the wounds and welts of the road.

"Wisdom," I remarked, in that silly, silent way of mine that employs ideas instead of words, "comes in just this way, in unusual clarity. The sun of Your wisdom is always shining, always radiant, always powerful; but we seldom expose ourselves to it. We prefer to let it sift down to us through the clouds of our worries, our fears, our cares, or our pride in the intellect You gave us. If we always let Your wisdom light our paths, what miracles of loveliness we should see!"

"There is an egg," You said. "Pick it up."

"Thank You, Lord," I said.

I picked it up, and held it a long time, admiring it. I liked the exquisite lines You had given it. I liked its size. It was bigger than a robin's egg, smaller than a pullet's.

I knew anyway that no robin had laid it there. It wasn't a robin's egg blue. By sheer coincidence, every robin's egg I ever saw has been a robin's egg blue. This egg was almost the color of a hen's.

I wondered whose it was. A crow's? A blue jay's? A grackle's? A woodpecker's? An owl's? I didn't know what color eggs they laid.

I didn't know what to do with the egg. That is, not exactly. I intended to take it home. I could put it in front of the statue of the Infant of Prague. What else can you do with an egg so wretchedly abandoned?

I was carrying a basket of stones. I couldn't entrust this lovely egg, this delicate shelled womb, to such dangerous companions.

I was sure the egg had life in it. It wasn't exactly warm; but it wasn't cold either. Its mother had flown away only a few minutes before You showed it to me—or so I thought.

I had pockets, but I had seen too many cartoons about men with eggs in their pockets. I wasn't going to be a man in a cartoon.

While I was trying to unscramble my brains, the egg dropped from my fingers and stained the road a brighter yellow.

Then it didn't matter what sort of bird the egg might have become.

It would never fly.

It would never enchant a man with a song.

It would never delight some child with its plumage.

It would never alight on the windowsill of some shut-in's bedroom and thank him for the crumbs his nurse had left there.

It would never help the trees in their fight against the insect pests that threatened to destroy them.

How many other lovely eggs I have smashed—eggs Your love and wisdom laid for me! Ideas You showed me in the night. I let them fall because I was too indolent to get up and write them down.

Those gifts, Lord, will never make Your children laugh or cry; feel pity or remorse or sympathy or love; taste consolation or hope or the desire for a better life.

They are, like the bird's egg, merely uncooked omelets lying on a stony road.

Once You permitted me to slip from Your fingers, but You did not let me smash.

I flew over the shabby hills and hollows of my life, a path similar to this road.

There I found not an egg alone, but also Your Holy Grail—from which I still sip greedily.

That Holy Grail was Marie. She was full of wine and honey, Lord. Sweet white wine; sweet wild honey.

You knocked the delicious cup aside and I was appalled. And angered.

It was not Your will that dropped me, Lord. It was mine. The will You gave me.

I fell, but You saved me from crashing to the ground.

You did not leave me there on the road for the sun to spoil and the rains to wash away. You did not desert me.

You gave me the Grail again in which I could quench my thirst for beauty and love and adventure—the golden wine and the honeyed spice of Mildred.

And when You took that away, You gave it back to me through Catherine.

The nectar of Catherine!

Cold drops of rain fell on me as I continued on. The sun had been shining only a minute ago. The sky above the spot where I found the egg now looked as though it had been scalped.

Its bald spot was immediately above me. A serene blue.

But around the baldness there were tufts of white and black and dirty gray.

The rain stopped. The sun came out again. The sky was blue again.

And I saw a wide wound in the road with small red bits of feldspar lying in it, winking at me, calling to me:

"Put thy fingers hither into my side; and be not faithless but believing."

I filled my basket with stones and my mind with the lost contents of the egg.

Faith falls like that egg, sometimes. And faith is much lovelier and more filling than any egg.

Faith, God, is one of Your most precious gifts. But it must be kept warm until it hatches. It must be nourished until it learns to fly and sing.

It must be fed with love.

Faith without good works is dead.

Faith without love is faith without a heart—for it is the heart that produces all good works.

Faith without a heart is as dead as the egg my clumsy fingers dropped.

Faith must not lie sterile in its shell. It must take on life.

It must grow until it can make the whole world rejoice in its splendor, its simplicity, and its exultant song.

Faith must put on wings.

Faith must learn to sing!

"I do believe, Lord; help Thou my unbelief."

Psalm 7

The oftener I see You, the closer I come to You.

The closer I come to You, the more I love You.

If I should ignore You, I could never adore You.

I forget You for hours but You never forget me for one moment.

It is human to forget and human to remember. And sometimes, memories of You so overwhelm me that they crowd my heart.

I remember You especially in flowers.

Acres and acres of pink and white and red carnations bobbing and bowing in the breeze, prostrating themselves before You and filling the earth with the spicy fragrance of their breath.

Flowers brought to my room by the girls who tend the garden.

A water lily floating in the swamp.

A country lane hemmed with Queen Anne's lace.

A stately row of hollyhocks and sunflowers and fire-blue shafts of larkspur peering at me over the top of a friendly fence and giving me Your regards.

Ropes of wistaria climbing up the balconies in Haifa, Israel.

A bit of edelweiss ambushed on a cloud-veiled mountain peak.

A humble blue flower looking at me from a prairie in Wisconsin as I sat by the window of the Narrow Gauge train that had stopped for a few moments for no good reason. I wanted to leap off the train and pick that flower but I was afraid the train would go without me.

I have been sorry ever since, and the memory of the flower, Your flower, still remains unplucked in my mind and in my heart.

It was a love letter from You. I never opened the envelope. I never read what You had written but I treasure the memory after more than sixty years.

There are so many other love letters from You that I cherish!

The night the Atlantic Ocean burst into flames, for instance.

I was in a plane high above the water. Something woke me. I looked down, half asleep, to see the ocean blazing.

I was astounded, for a wonderful moment, at so great a miracle.

I saw the red flames leaping up everywhere to fall back on the surface in golden splendor.

And suddenly I realized that this was only the mirror of the rising sun and the plane must be somewhere close to Amsterdam.

The Joshua trees in Arizona and the long desert stretches of sand and stone and lava dust and hills and valleys filled with Your own jewelry—bits of trees that have turned through many centuries into glorious rock.

The pomegranate I watched every day during my retreat in the convent garden of the Little Sisters of Jesus, the daughters of Charles de Foucauld in Nazareth of Galilee.

But I love You best, I think, in the people, living and dead, You have mailed to me.

I love the faces I see wherever I go.

Lord, why do You surround me with saints, Your very holy chosen ones? I find them everywhere; and they are more miraculous than the spice of the carnation, or the glory of apple trees in bloom.

And I wonder why You have chosen me!

Nuns and priests have left the Church to the scandal of many, but there are multitudes of saints who still remain in Your tents.

If wine is the laughter of the peasant girls of France, or Italy, or Portugal, or Spain, the laughter in Your convents and Your seminaries is the wine of holiness. And I have sipped it often.

I remember a houseful of nuns and novices whose coifs were so shining white, they made me think of white caps rushing in on me at high tide.

No two convents are alike, yet each has its own rich laughter, its own real joy, its own distinctive sweetness and savor.

I saw a nun in a convent in Alabama who asked me to pray for the soul of her mother and gave me a prayer she might have written out of her heart—it is so simple and lovely.

"We consecrate to Thee, O Jesus of love, the trials and

the joys and the happiness of our family life, and we beseech Thee to pour out Thy blessings on all its members, absent and present, living and dead. And when, one after the other, we shall have fallen asleep in Thy blessed bosom, may all of us, in Paradise, find again our family united in Thy Sacred Heart. Amen."

"Jesus of love!" Have You ever heard anything nicer, God?

That nun's mother, that lovely blessed ghost whom I never met, is close to me now, day and night. So many men and women I never knew came into my life after theirs had ended. These, with others I knew and love, comprise "my gang."

May they be waiting at the depot when I come!

Lord, I love all Your spices for they put zest and excitement and aroma and pleasure into my life.

Now, why, in spite of all the saints I know and love, do I still remain a sinner?

You have chosen me crazy as it seems. I too am Yours! You will take care of me! You will be with me, though I go through fire and water, through terrors and trials.

You have loved me with an everlasting love. And I have loved You—a little, in my fashion.

I am a cold gray stone reflecting not the light of the sun but the infinite glory of the Maker of all the suns that are!

Why isn't my reflection brighter?

I still hope, Lord. I know I shall not be forsaken; for many saints are praying for me all over the earth. And saints and angels in "my gang" are praying for me too. With their help, I "got it made." They will make sure that this faint glimmer will not wear off, even if it never gets any "brighter."

Those white-capped novices are gathering oceans of love and prayers to wash me to the shores of heaven.

Why should I feel "scared"?

How silly it is not to be a saint! How damned silly, God!

Your hand is in mine. I shall not be afraid.

*Psalm 8*

*Lord, there is no one mightier than You.*

There is no one holier than You.

There is no one in heaven or earth who is anywhere nearly so beautiful as You.

And every day Your might and Your holiness and Your power become a part of me.

Every day Your divine flesh becomes part of me. Your divine blood rushes through my arteries and veins and pumps through my heart.

Yet I remain a weakling and a sinner.

Is my skin still so covered with the unholy oils of the world that it sheds the rain of Your blessings and keeps my heart dust-dry?

Must I always fight You, God?

Must I always wrestle with You as Jacob wrestled with the angel and limp away to my snide and shoddy triumphs?

Every day heaven renews my body and cleans and stirs my blood.

Every day You give my soul glorious new life and I am still an ugly sinner.

Is my free will—the will You gave me in my mother's womb—more powerful than Yours, Almighty God?

Why do I feast on You; why do I fill myself with You and remain a spineless worm?

Is my reason greater than Your Wisdom, or am I just a normal human man?

You came down from heaven to bring heaven to us and us to heaven.

And we mocked You. We made a clown of You.

We gave You a phony sceptre and a phony crown.

We spit in Your face and tortured You and killed You.

Must I spit in Your face every day, and must I kill You?

Why do my triumphs over You never give me joy?

Why do they always make me unhappy and ashamed?

Why do I always feel like a child who has cheated his father in a friendly game of checkers?

Lord, I own no single inch of soil but You have given me title and deed to all Your heaven and to all Your earth, to have and to hold, so long as You reign.

All my life You have given me Christmas presents, for

every day is Christmas Day with You.

You have given me gifts I can never fully appreciate, including the gold and frankincense and myrrh of my three marriages.

And I have given You nothing but myself.

One day we did not fight.

One day I was all Yours.

One day You were My All.

One October day some years ago I felt I had made up to You for all my mean and vicious and sly and cunning sins.

God, cunning has more force than violence; and slyness is far more malevolent than pure hate.

It was my seventy-fifth birthday and I had been promised the supreme privilege of drinking from the chalice at the late afternoon Mass.

For hours I walked through Your valleys and Your hills. Wherever I trod, the milkweed pod and the goldenrod, with every curtsy and bow and nod, helped me to sing Your praises, God.

It was a solemn day, but who could be entirely solemn in the splendor of Your autumn world?

Trees that were so glorious with color a few weeks ago—"Terrible as an army with banners"—looked like a battlefield. Only a few flags hovered here and there over the dying and the dead.

The bare black branches of the maples and the oaks lifted in mourning put a fringe on the blue surface of the sky.

I watched the dead leaves struggling in the little creek. They were spreading and speeding my love for You down to the river, down to the sea.

I knew the sun would lift their love up to the sky and the sky would carry it to You.

Everything was gay the whole day long, gay as a little black and white dog who went rushing into the woods every now and then for a sniff of this and a sniff of that and came rushing back to me again.

My heart was young and gay and filled with love as I knelt on the prie-dieu near the altar.

I imagined myself to be on Calvary waiting for someone to bring me the cup, the Holy Grail, with the

Blood and Water from the wounded Heart of Christ. And I was thinking of the crucifixion and the curious fact that there can be great joy in suffering of great pain.

The joy does not begin with the first blow, nor with the second, nor with the third.

There are three dreadful moments for each blow: the moment the eye beholds the hammer lifted before it strikes; the moment the spike is driven deeply through the flesh; and the moment when the hammer is lifted and the full shock of pain takes possession not only of the wound but of the entire body.

Then one looks down at Mary and the pain turns into joy unutterable, for this is really something fit to offer God.

It can be given in part-payment for all the debts we owe and the debts of all our enemies and friends and people we do not know—the lonely, the wretched, the leper, the cripple, the hungry, the convict, the trollop, and the tramp.

All too suddenly it was communion time.

My prie-dieu was carried to the front of the altar and I received the Host. Then the priest went back to the altar and returned to me with the Chalice. I took it in both hands and lifted it to my lips.

Today almost everybody takes the Chalice in his hands as though it were not a privilege but a right. But this was years ago.

Light filled the cup as I raised it. A light brighter than the sun. Golden wine in a golden cup. The light filled the world.

Sunrise, sunset, and the sky with no horizon, no clouds, no anything but light.

Light poured into me with the wine—the wine that had been changed into the very Blood of Christ.

And love poured into me with the light.

Love directly from the Source of Love.

A Niagara of love and light. It overwhelmed not only me, it overwhelmed the chapel, it overwhelmed the earth.

Why can't that day come back again, Lord, and stay with me?

Why can't I remember every day that You are Love

and Light and Power, Beauty and Wisdom and Grace
and that I need You every minute, every hour?

Lord, do not always let me win, for if I win too often I
shall lose You and all Your earth and heaven.

Give me back my seventy-fifth birthday every day.

Psalm 9

I am trying to set them down so I will not forget them. I forget so easily the marvellous words You pour into my ears.

You give me handfuls of pearls and I let them fall before the swine. I am quite unreliable, but I love You just the same.

I was walking through the neck-high ferns making a path through them with my crooked stick hoping to find a redtop mushroom underneath the ferns.

I wasn't really interested in collecting mushrooms yesterday. It was chokecherries I wanted.

"The ferns are too high and mighty," You said. "No mushroom could get the light and the warmth of My sun with ferns so high above them—any more than My children can get My light and My warmth from preachers and writers who grow too tall for them.

"These ferns are living for their own glory. They think I made the world for ferns. They do not think of sheltering such little things as mushrooms."

"Mushrooms need ferns, though," I said to You. (I should tell You!)

"Or they need blackberry vines, or little pine trees, or sumacs that grow near the poplar groves. They must have something to keep the sun from hitting them directly and burning them up.

Just so, we need preachers and writers to temper Your messages for us. Only someone like Moses could listen to You face to face. Only the saints, the great doctors of the Church, the mystics and the humble ones can bring You down to our littleness."

I went to a spot where the ferns were only knee-high and I found a perfect mushroom. Thank You, Lord. Afterwards I found another 'neath the dark green hem of a seedling spruce.

There weren't any others worth picking, so I decided to go on.

I wanted the chokecherries, not for jams or jellies or pies or wine. I wanted them for dyeing. I have become a nut about natural dyes.

I gather all kinds of things, and one of our girls turns

them into dyes. It is surprising what happens.

For instance, the bright maroon sumac combs made a dull brown dye. The strawberries made, first, a pale pink shade, then one almost an orange red.

Blueberries made violet dye in one experiment and dark green in a second.

The white tops and the green stems and leaves of the yarrow plant made a light green tint, whereas the white tops processed by themselves made a shady yellow.

Milkweed blossoms, fireweed, purple vetch, and other plants made various shades of green.

One of the lichens we tried gave us an orange color.

Daisies dyed yellow. The flowers of the devil's paint-brush furnished us a warm pink-brown.

The goldenrod gave us a goldenrod hue. It was the only specimen that yielded what was expected of it.

You know what happened to all the purple clover tops. We dyed a white wool sweater of mine. It came out of the bath a rare yellow-green. I have never seen anything like that shade, not in the last seventy years. I wouldn't take $1,000 for that sweater. It is the most beautiful one on earth!

When I put it on, I put on fields and fields and fields of clover, flights of dusty bumblebees, a million lovely and healing fragrances, Your sunshine, Your clean winds, Your winding country roads, Your eternal hills—the clouds of butterflies below and the clutter of flying clouds above.

I was thinking of that sweater as I milked the choke-cherry tree. I was wondering what color dye, if any, the chokecherries would make. Some of those berries were a bright red, some a dark red, some a coffee color.

"Lord," I said, "this little tree has a hundred times as many udders as any cow. How come? And it gives wine instead of milk. Which has the more vitamins, chokecherry wine or milk?"

You didn't answer that last question because You knew I didn't care, didn't really want an answer.

You knew I would drink anything You sent my way, even Scotch.

While I was filling my basket, I saw something I never noticed before. It was a strikingly beautiful wad that had been stuck or pasted on a twig.

It had a glaze. It looked like black wax sprinkled with gold dust and powdered emeralds. It had a luster. It glittered in the sunlight like a rare jewel.

It was, of course, the nursery of some type of worm or caterpillar or insect unknown to me.

Some lowly creature had laid it there and it contained, perhaps, half a million eggs. This was something no bigger than a good-sized mass of chewing gum!

I snipped off one of the twigs so signally ornamented, and took it home.

I looked at the wad through a magnifying glass and found something resembling a honeycomb.

A mass of tiny cells! Each cell filled with life waiting its time to begin!

Lord, You cannot help revealing Your love even for wasps or bees or ants—or whatever sort of parasites are concealed in this lump.

You spin beautiful cocoons for caterpillars.

You put divine color and design and pattern and ingenuity into everything You make.

You put as much splendor and love into this amazing mass as You put into Your stars.

And there is efficiency too! When those hungry little monsters are due to come out of their waiting room, their superbly appointed and enamelled world, breakfast will be waiting for them.

A "coming-out party" divinely ordained! The tender bark of the tree. The soft green leaves (or maybe an old brown withered leaf for roughage).

Perhaps, even an old leftover chokecherry to nibble on. And no nonsense about proteins or carbohydrates.

You surround these pests, whatever they are, with infinite tenderness!

Why then did You ordain that Your Son should be born in a stinking stable in a cold and rocky cave?

You answered me with questions.

"Should I have let Him begin life in a palace?

"In an inn?

"Or in a hospital where He and His Mother would have every care?

"Did I not want Him to be a poor man, like other poor

men? Do you not know that I love poor men?

"Did I not want Him to know all the woes and joys of poor men?

"Of course the cave in Bethlehem wasn't as beautiful, nor as cozy and snug, nor as well-planned, as that larval smear that has attracted you; but were not Mary and Joseph there to tend Him?

"Could you have done better for Him?

"Could even I, God, have done better for Him?"

While I was thinking how to answer You, You said:

"Besides, My Son can rely on the love of many people. Centuries and centuries of people.

"He can look after them, but only I can look after the least of these, My creatures."

Thank You, God, for bothering with the likes of me.

The waiting room, or smear, or larval nursery, which I have made for my own "coming-out party" is crude and clumsy and messy and chaotic, compared with the unknown monsters'.

I need You too.

I need You more than any other insect does.

With Your grace I can do better.

I would like to milk your graces out of heaven into the basket of my soul, as I milked the chokecherry trees.

As for my "coming-out party"—I leave it all to You.

Fix up any kind of smear for me, or any sort of stable, palace, or whatever else You like. And any kind of banquet You see fit to arrange for me.

It will be more than I expect and more than I deserve.

*Dear God, to Whom all flesh must come, I confess I listened to the scolding of the squirrel rather then to the solemn and splendid words of the priest.*

I had heard those words so many times, always above the coffin of someone dear to me.

The words have been etched by daggers into my poor human mind and I was not in the mood for solemnity or eloquence or words of any kind.

In Greece and Russia, in Israel and the Arab countries, the priest and the choirs sing Alleluias at all the Requiem Masses, "Alleluia, Alleluia, Alleluia."

A citizen of some poor little mountain parish has become a glorious saint in heaven, "Alleluia, Alleluia, Alleluia."

There was no gaiety here, nor joy, nor even any laughter.

I like the Irish wakes that I attended when I was a boy. There was always laughter there, as well as tears, and there were funny and fascinating stories as well as prayers. Also there were always pretty girls.

The squirrel was showering curses on the funeral crowd. It had come too close to the tree in which she had gathered her whole year's savings of hazelnuts and acorns and other treasures.

It was the squirrel who made me remember Gid most clearly.

Gid was a great fisherman, a mighty hunter, the guide of many tourists in the spring and fall, and the greatest and most lovable liar in the land.

He loved to tell lies as he sat around the campfire at night cooking dinner, gutting fish, or maybe skinning a deer.

And he spoke to make the men around him feel kinship with one another. The stories they tell of him are many.

"How do you spell 'squirrels?'" one of his clients asked him.

"One *i* and two *r's*," another man replied.

A red-faced man, a wealthy Cleveland lawyer, took exception to that remark.

"The squirrel has two eyes, everybody knows. Look at those two in the elm tree over there. Each of them has two eyes."

"How much do you want to bet?" Gid asked. "The female has no right eye and the husband has no left."

The lawyer laughed at him.

"How can you tell the female from the male at this distance?"

"Which one is doing all the scolding?" Gid asked him.

"Get your gun and bring 'em both down," the lawyer said; "bet you twenty dollars each has two eyes."

"You're covered," Gid said, and said "bang, bang" with the gun.

The squirrels dropped down at his feet.

Gid picked them up and showed them to the lawyer.

"The twenty bucks is mine," he said. "You see, this squirrel has no right eye, this one no left."

The lawyer laughed and put the money in Gid's hand.

"I bet you fifty you can't do that again," he said.

"Mister," Gid replied, "we don't waste squirrel meat around here. These two will make a stew that will last us for the next three days. All I need is some potatoes, a few slices of old salt pork, some fiddlehead ferns—this is the season for them—and all the morels you can find."

"What's a morel?"

"It's a type of mushroom," Gid explained, "and very tasty if one knows how to cook it."

Gid served his country in two wars. So a number of tired old soldiers were here in the graveyard, paying the last honors to their comrade.

Gid would have loved this mourning, this graveyard, this gathering of old friends.

It was a perfect August day. The clouds had just been taken from their cupboard. They were still new, still clean.

The blue sky wore them proudly.

The wind had perfumed itself with many odors: trees and wild flowers and the grass that had been crushed by many feet; the new-turned earth; and the fresh young cones which the pine trees had sprinkled around the grave.

They were a soft green, those cones; they were elongated crescents. They looked like so many little green fish with gold and silver icing on the edges of their scales where the resin had begun to ooze. They smelled as though they had been dipped in turpentine before they kissed the earth.

A tall old maple that overlooked the graveyard and the river was flying crimson flags that most trees save until the autumn comes.

Gid Rose, old soldier, old hunter and trapper, old fisherman and guide, old friend and neighbor, had one particular lie he loved to tell. It was being buried with him.

At the end of the day when the fish had not been biting, or the deer had not come near them, he loved to sit the men down and spin his lies to their delight.

To every new batch of men he guided, he told with proper gestures the story of his posthole joys and sorrows.

"Them postholes used to lie around loose everywhere and I was always worrying about 'em. Postholes deteriorate if a man don't take care of 'em.

"You can't bring 'em inside the house. There's no room for 'em. You gotta leave 'em outside.

"It's tough to sit up all night with a lantern and watch over 'em like a shepherd over his sheep.

"Rain and snow and dead leaves and loose stones can get into 'em.

"Sometimes dogs sniff around 'em. Sometimes a passing skunk stops to say 'hello' to 'em."

Fish were frying as Gid talked—as the priest continued with his eulogy.

Twigs were sputtering and snapping in the campfire. Smoke was blending with the dusk. Gid was standing tall and straight and solemn, holding a fork in his powerful right hand, squinting a little—because of the smoke—at the men sitting all around him listening to his talk.

"No, I didn't mean to put fenceposts in 'em holes. Don't need a fence.

"I collected 'em like some of you fellas collect dollar bills.

"Posthole crazy! But, easy come, easy go.

"Man goes to sleep a posthole millionaire, and wakes to find himself a beggar.

"One night, while I was dreaming about owning all the postholes in Canada, a wind blew up and filled everyone of my holes with sand.

"Couldn't identify one of 'em. I was wiped out!"

"What did you want to do with your postholes, anyway?" someone was sure to ask.

"You never know when them holes will come in handy. Get enough of 'em together, you can make yourself a tunnel, or a well, or a mine, or, maybe, for all I know, a lot of foxholes or a couple of miles of trenches."

"Shut up," I told the squirrel.

Gid Rose was a living symbol of Canada.

He had its majesty, its strength, its bigness, its grace, its rugged honesty, its sublime simplicity, its wealth of energy, and all its gaiety and fun.

He didn't die broke. He still had postholes.

He had as many postholes as he had medals on his uniform jacket, enough to furnish him a deep and wide and comfortable and everlasting grave.

Take care of him, Lord.

He was, in his own way, one of the most religious men I knew. He could not say with the psalmist:

"I have loved, O Lord, the beauty of Thy house and the place where Thy glory dwelleth."

But he could say that he loved the garden of that house, Your Own great out-of-doors.

Introduce him to Peter, Lord, and let them talk about the fish they caught and the fish that got away.

When the priest had finished, the old soldiers went one by one close to the grave. They saluted solemnly, then each returned to his place to stand at attention while the bugle sounded Taps.

A blue jay screamed just once somewhere behind and high above the graveyard.

Gid would certainly have loved that unexpected and most beautiful Requiem. It held all the joy and all the Alleluias I had missed.

Psalm 11

*Dear God, Creator of eternity and time and tides, gray*
*days have overcome me and I lie in bed, inert and*
*useless, and in some little pain.*

The heaviness of the atmosphere outside threatens to
squeeze the arteries and veins that pump the red blood
through my heart—my blood that is mixed with Yours!

Nurses with pills and punctures attend me day and
night. And a bottle of good, red Scotch sits near my hand
ready at an instant to dilate those arteries and veins the
weather threatens, and to keep the red blood coursing
through me.

And time and tide go washing through me too,
changing yesterdays into today and todays into yesterdays.

What is time to You or me?

What is yesterday to You or me?

No yesterday is dead so long as it is remembered.

So on this gray day I walk with my brother Bill again
on the shores of Long Beach, California.

It is too cold for us to swim, so we wade.

We walk a mile or so enjoying Your wind and Your
sun and Your surf and the wet sands beneath our feet
and the wide expanse of the blue, blue sea and the
unlimited tent of blue above us.

The sky is full of gulls, white and swift and screaming.

The shore is full of shells and driftwood and bits of
seaweed and crazy crabs that scuttle backward.

And the sea is full of whitecaps that are noisier and
whiter and more graceful than the gulls.

There is a fog, not over the beach but over the water.

There is a freighter anchored not far away. It looks
like some giant insect caught and held in a master
spider's web.

There is a ghostly pier thrusting itself into the sea
about a mile or so to the right of us with some vague
smoke-wrapped, gray-blurred buildings on it. And there
is a foghorn somewhere that bewails its fate every few
minutes.

I talk to You, Lord, more often than I talk to Bill.

"You have washed my dirty feet with Your mighty
ocean, even as Your Son washed the feet of Judas and
the others. Keep them clean and busy on Your errands."

**48** We absorb the ocean of Your love as the sand absorbs the sea. Where the waves have wet it, the sand is soft but solid. It is easy to walk upon.

Higher up above the waterline the sand is as hard as concrete.

A little higher still, it is as loose and unreliable as the wind.

When we are saturated with Your love we may comfort the barefooted world. Men may trample on us leaving deep or shallow impressions. They may see Your goodness as they go their way.

In a moment, new waves of Your love will erase all footprints and leave only Yourself—only Yourself and me.

You and me—stand waiting for the next bare feet or the next heavy brogues. Or perhaps, the next pair of high-heeled shoes.

You said, "I made the sands as well as the water. I made both for you and yours.

"You have walked My sands for many years, but how often have you waded or swum in the ocean of My love?

"You live on the shore of the sea of eternity, the tides lap the sands of your life. Someday they will wash that sand deep into My heart."

I said aloud, "The humility and the compassion of my God!"

It pleased me to think of You patiently rubbing mountains together to make all the beaches in the world.

We came back to the beach next day, Bill and I.

The sun was shining brightly. There were millions of bird tracks on the shore.

Jet planes were chalk-marking the heavens. The sky was smudged here and there with lampblack.

A man was throwing bread crumbs to the birds.

Gulls were flying in all directions, as crowds to a red-flag orator.

The air was full of wings, the tide was out and the only sound we heard was the mooing, cooing, wooing of the birds and, of course, the distant organ thunder of Your Pacific Sea.

I said, "Lord, it is good to be here. It is good to see Your name on so many things."

I pick up a pebble, it says, "God."
I pick up a piece of driftwood: "God."

Your name is stamped on the sand, the kelp, the birds, the people around us, the pier, the rusty freighter, the water, the sun, and the little boats that skim across the waves.

Even the smell of sea is stamped with Your signature and the words "Made in Heaven."

You said, "You two, you and your brother Bill, and all the children of man, were made in heaven, for heaven. You all are stamped with My name. You are a child of God.

"Talk to My other children; tell them about Me.

"Most of them have forgotten Me or have never heard of Me. Some do not know that I exist.

"Some believe that I am dead.

"Tell them I have survived all their death notices and always shall.

"Tell them to wade in the sea of My mercy while they may."

As I lie here now, Your love rushes at me like the surf.

It hammers at me just like the lines of white water charging through the blue and the green, to smash into foaming rainbows all around me.

We cannot escape Your love even though we try.

That is a terrible truth, the almost unbelievable truth.

Why do You love us so?

Why do You give Your seashells such beauty? I remember one with a rattlesnake design. It had a doorway that glowed with the lustre of a pearl. The creature who owned it had a house more lovely, more snug, more artfully designed than the Taj Mahal.

That creature lived in the depths of the ocean. It could not appreciate the beauty nor the simplicity nor the sublimity of itself and its house, nor be aware of the Divine Wisdom that gave it life and living.

If You love that senseless shellfish so much, how much more do You love man!

*Psalm 12*

*Lord Jesus, Who said, "Suffer the little children to come unto Me and forbid them not, for of such is the kingdom of God," I am glad that You were born when and where You were.*

I am glad that You were not born in these beloved United States of Yours.

Nor in these godless times.

What would happen if the Angel Gabriel appeared to a little girl in Keokuk, Kankakee or Kalamazoo, or some place in the coal fields of Kentucky? Suppose he had a message for her from God Himself.

The little girl would probably not know what he meant.

For God has become an ugly three-letter word that must never be spoken aloud in our public schools in the presence of innocent children.

He would probably talk of "divine providence" or "fate." He might even refer to You as "the man upstairs" or as "Mr. Biggest."

The little girl would agree to be the mother of the king who would save the whole world and herself and her family, but when the curves of pregnancy began to appear, Papa and Mama would become alarmed.

They would question her about "the man upstairs" and they would not believe a thing she said. They might call in a pet psychologist who would not make the little girl change her mind.

Then they would call in good old Dr. Gray, who had saved Mama seven times from bearing an unwanted child.

You Lord, might be emptied into the nearest sewer!

And there would be no salvation for the world.

Mama and Papa will explain to You at the wrong time and the wrong place that her virgin's honor must be kept alive and glorified, even though it too has been aborted.

They will explain that a bride must always wear white silk and satin at her wedding—at least at her first wedding—to show the world that she is a true virgin.

The times have changed much since Your day, Lord. An adulteress is no longer stoned to death. Often she is bedecked with diamonds and rubies and emeralds and with ropes of pearls.

Sometimes she acts on the stage or on the movie screen or in a television skit. And millions and millions of people applaud.

An abortion is no longer an abomination, strange as that may seem. Many honorable and righteous men have made it free and legal and the right of every girl and woman in the land.

The word now is that "every woman has the right of her own body and may do with it what she will."

The people who coined this particular phrase, Lord, also will explain it in their own way when You ask them about it.

Be patient, Lord, and You will learn quite a lot about women's rights in this modern age.

Abortion is done scientifically now, Lord, and without too much mangling or butchering. And the doctors in many hospitals throughout the land who are appointed to this task are all honorable men.

They may not like the work they do, but they get to think of it as their duty. And, perhaps, they reason that what they do is a "far, far better thing than they have ever done before," and that it is much better to sacrifice an unwanted and unwelcome baby than a wanted and much welcome dollar.

The price is high now, Lord. Not just thirty pieces of silver.

And a clever doctor can live well on his practice. He will explain his motives to You and his reasons in due time, when the dark angel ushers him from your waiting room into Your private office for his final examination.

Lord, how many children were slaughtered by King Herod?

How many by our modern medicos and the papas and mamas of young girls? And by married and unmarried women and their husbands or their lovers?

How many hundreds of millions of souls would be born into Your kingdom if those unwanted babies had been allowed to live?

How many potential saints has the kingdom of heaven lost?

How many geniuses, musicians, actors, statesmen, poets, and heroes have been denied to Your United

You see, Lord, our intellectuals, our so-called eggheads or big shots have decided that You have lost Your grip, that You have let the population of the world slip too far from Your control.

They figure, with their higher mathematics and their omnipotent computers, that unless they stop You, You will put six billion people on this world.

Far too many to feed, to clothe, to shelter, to educate and to use!

We still observe the anniversary of Your birth each year.

Little groups of Your friends go here and there singing hymns about the little town of Bethlehem.

But the big business is that of Santa Claus and his eight reindeer. The big stores in the great thoroughfares of the major cities of the world are all for Santa Claus and not for You. Santa Claus means big business.

The merchants will explain all this to You, each in his own way, when they come to the gates of Your kingdom.

Christmas is not really Christmas time, just as Easter is no longer the day of the Resurrection but the day of the Easter Bunny, a rabbit who lays hard-boiled eggs, hens' eggs, of various colors, and hides them where little children, who know not God, can find them.

Maybe I look at this thing in a wrong light, Lord Jesus.

Maybe I should see only that the honorable, the righteous, the eminent and the rich are dwindling and dwindling and dwindling through the abortion they have authorized and made so free.

And it is the poor and the needy, the ordinary and the humble people of the world who still bear children for the kingdom of God.

Maybe in time, Your own time, God, the advocates of abortion will all have vanished from the world.

And the world will be Yours again.

In the land of the free—free love, free adultery, "free" abortion—we teach sex in our public schools; we teach birth control; planned parenthood—which means "We plan not to be parents"—and contraceptives. We teach hygiene; and we exalt the pill. The pill has become as popular as heroin or marijuana.

We teach hygiene, but never holiness nor reverence nor religion.

We teach sports and games, but never the happiness of loving God.

We teach technologies and trades, but never love or peace or prayers or any sort of virtue.

And we teach common sense, or should I say human wisdom, which is not wisdom at all.

"Why should Meg abandon her art classes, her tennis and her bridge games to wrestle with diapers and dishes in a kitchen full of flies?"

"And why should Mick walk the floor with a crying baby every night when he could be studying the hieroglyphics of some new star or planet science has discovered in some far galaxy of Your heaven?"

Science is science; there is no God but science, and astronomers are His prophets.

The astronauts have found the moon and trampled over it, and played golf upon its surface, and picked up rocks, and planted flags and left them there.

There was a time when man fought and died in bloody wars because they thought the moon was a god and they were devoted to it and to its adoration. And science has proved the moon is not a god and those who thought it was are merely stupid savages.

"The moon is not a god," they will tell you again and again, and they will add, "There is no God."

They know the moon is there; they know its movements are fixed forever and ever, but they will not admit it was created and flung into space and orbit by its Creator.

Lord, have mercy on us!

Psalm 13

*My heart is peaceful today, Lord, as peaceful as the hills*
*behind me, as peaceful as the beach on which I walk, or*
*the clouds that move so effortlessly above.*

My heart is as filled and as restless and as joyous as
the ocean I see all about me; for You have shown me
love, both human and divine.

Yesterday a missionary nurse took me in her ancient
Ford car to a distant clinic in which she works. We made
one stop on the way, for she had to attend a patient.

"There's no shade here," she said, "and I don't think
you want to wait in the car. You have no idea how hot it
can get. I'll ask one of the women to let you sit in the
shade someplace."

There was a cluster of little wooden houses; and
women in all of them. The men were working somewhere, out on the sea, perhaps, or maybe on the roads.
And there were children everywhere. I was welcomed
into a house by three of the ladies, one of them a granny.

They gave me a comfortable chair and saw that I had
plenty of air. One of the women turned on the radio.
There was little talk. We looked at each other, smiled,
and kept silent—but it was plain we were friends.
Anybody with the nurse was a friend in this place.

The missionary struggled up a hillside to the home of
her patient, carrying two kit bags. Nursing stuff, I
imagine. She went up easily, as though she had climbed
rugged mountains all her life.

I rejoiced in the wind, the cleanliness of the room, the
beauty of some of the children who came running in and
went running out again, and at the pictures on the walls.

A framed picture of a bride and groom, the bride in a
long full wedding dress. A lithograph of the English
royal family. Several pictures of the Blessed Virgin.

Chickens came clucking in, to be immediately swished
out by the granny. Cotton was growing outside the window. And palm trees were waving not far away from
where I sat.

The granny disappeared and returned presently with
three eggs. These she put in a paper bag, twisting the top
and then folding it down; she put the bag on top of a tall
arrangement of shelves that suggested a bookcase, a
china cabinet, or something of the sort.

The nurse came down, running as usual, and announced that mother and child were doing well. A little girl came running after her, holding a paper bag which she insisted on giving to the missionary—despite the fact that her hands were full. Then granny gave me the paper bag of eggs and smiled, and shook my hands as though I were the president of the world. I guessed there were eggs in the nurse's paper bag too. There were.

A dozen or more patients were sitting outside the clinic when I arrived, waiting their turns. A little girl had a bad cut over her right eye. An elderly woman lay on the bench, full length, as though she were about to die. There were several men with bandages on their bare feet or arms. And there were children with nothing apparently wrong with them.

Toward noon a woman of eighty or so came walking slowly to the clinic, aided by a long, slim sapling someone had recently cut for her. She was just able to make the one step up to the porch.

When the last patient, the very old lady, had been treated, the nurse opened the doors of her little car; seven or eight men and women managed to squeeze in. The very old lady was the first to enter, with the help of the others. When the nurse let her out, she gave the nurse two eggs in a paper bag.

"Even the poorest of the poor wants to give you something," she said.

I already knew that, Lord. You had made that very plain to me.

"And you dare not refuse, for it is given out of the heart."

We went home as fast as the law permitted—fifteen miles per hour—the missionary pointing out the houses where she had delivered babies. She had to be part mountain goat to get to some of them.

"How many children I have brought into the world! How many nights I spent sleeping on the floor or in some strange bed, waiting for a child to be born, and how many wonderful people I have found here," she said, "I couldn't begin to tell."

I kept saying to myself, "If you love Me, you will love one another." I kept saying to myself, "Whatever you have done to the least of these, you have done unto Me."

And peace flooded me, Lord.

And today on these sands, You showed me another kind of love.

A little while ago three rowboats came dancing through the water. Fishermen leaped out of one of them and pulled a long net out of the water. I saw flashes of silver, like so many sparks of light.

I have seldom seen such beauty as that net enclosed—the fishes shining in the sun and the sand, in the wet meshes of the net.

A variety of living colors. Colors I couldn't believe at first. Simply because I saw them gleaming on the silver sides of fish.

Some had a blue that I had seen only once before, in a glacier in Alaska. Some had a green or orange or golden sheen. Two or three of them shone with a light that was almost purple.

All these vivid colors were flashing in the sun, and the silver was flashing too as the fishes jumped and squirmed and tried to escape.

"Jacks," an American tourist said proudly, "those are jacks. I love jacks." He meant he loved them fried. "What's that big fish with the long wicked snout?" a woman nearby asked him.

"Gars," the man said. "And the little one is a baby gar. Two sea-gars. Why don't you laugh? I said 'two sea-gars.' Where's your sense of humor?"

He pointed out several porcupine fish and half a dozen sea urchins, which look like balls of black and white and gray pins.

The net was hauled out from under the splendid shining, fighting, and dying pile of fish, the living fountain of glorious colored lights.

These beautiful jacks and the wicked gars and the ugly porcupine fish were mixed together in the sand; and men began to sort them and throw them into baskets so that they might be served somewhere as food.

Beauty, Lord, lives only for a moment, and then it's destroyed. But what a moment to live!

"This beauty," You said, "will feed My children, and that is beautiful and good."

**58** "But the greatest beauty ever born on earth, My Son, gave Himself to you and all the world for everlasting food."

Love, human and divine.

How can a mind be calm, Lord, and how can a heart that is peaceful and full of love act like the sea in a storm?

*You had no beginning, Lord.*

You can have no end.

Therefore, the story of Your romance with the lady of Nazareth can have neither beginning nor end.

But I like to think of it, looking through the long arches of the centuries, as beginning thousands of years ago when You stood by a brawling river, measuring the heights of the mountains and the depths of the oceans, and creating all kinds of animals, male and female, for the delight of the little girl at Your side.

She would not be born for centuries, but she was alive in Your mind and heart. And she was perfect. You being perfect never could resist perfection.

She was perfect because there was no stain of sin in her.

She was the flawless Eden You had designed for sinners.

She was to be Your queen, and the mother of Your Son!

She was the garden enclosed, the fountain sealed, in which You took delight.

I write, Lord, as a fool and a child, because that's what I am; and I write because I believe it is Your will that I write.

I have no visions. I have no mystic experiences. But thoughts come to me, on weary nights and painful days, out of talking with Our Lady and many of the saints.

"Immaculate! Immaculate! There is no stain in thee."

You could have made her immaculate by willing it, but I don't think You did it that way.

When someone loves divinely, He likes to go to a lot of trouble to give her the right ancestors and all that she needed.

Then, I think, You sent all the angels of heaven in procession to the home of Joachim and Anne, to be sure no human frailty menaced the tiny cell that would be the mother of Your Son.

Because I am a child and a fool, I can see the angels swinging golden censors, and I can smell the aroma of rich incense burning in them.

Once upon a time You built an Eden for Your children, but Adam and Eve destroyed it.

Mary, You knew, would be another Eden.

You also knew, through all eternity, that she was essential to the redemption of all men, because her will was Your will.

She obeyed You, through love, as completely as a rudder obeys the slightest wish of the hand that guides it.

You watched her grow in time, in wisdom, grace and holiness. She had more wisdom than Solomon. And the summit of her wisdom was that joy could come only through doing the will of God, even though that will should destroy her.

She knew also that he who follows his own will inevitably destroys himself.

You had the best masters in Israel teach her all that had been written about the Messiah and You inspired her to meditate on the role His mother must play in the drama of reconciliation.

I, Your retarded child, believe I hear her thinking, though she does not speak aloud:

"O most privileged lady, God the Holy Ghost will place in the chalice of your slim body the divinity of God the Son, and you will give Him birth!

"You will be the mother of God! Your womb will be His heaven on earth. You will feed Him, the Almighty, with the milk of your body. You will caress and kiss Him.

"What other human being ever held God in her arms and kissed Him?

"But oh, poor lady, poor lady! Life will be a long tragedy for you. For you know that He comes to be a holocaust.

"He must be tortured and killed and offered up to God for the sake of men; and you, poor lady, must offer Him as His Father does.

"You must not interfere with the bloody sacrifice. In fact, you must do all you can to see that the sacrifice is completed; and you must love all those who torture Him and kill Him, for they are your children.

"His Father is the Father of all men. His mother must be the mother of all men."

So when You, Lord, were ready to send Your angel to her, she was still mourning for the mother of the

Messiah.

She was startled at the angel's word, and quite confused.

How could she be the mother of the Messiah? She had
taken a vow of virginity.

The angel must know that. Wasn't it he who told her
God was a jealous God, and she must love no one but
Him?

"How can this be?" she asked, "since I am a virgin?"

"The Holy Spirit shall come upon you and the power
of the Most High will overshadow you!"

In that moment she remembered the Prophet Isaiah:
"Therefore the Lord himself will give you this sign: the
virgin shall be with child, and bear a son, and shall
name him Immanuel."

This confirmed the angel Gabriel's words. So, she herself was to be the mother of the Messiah!

Poor lady—poor lady!

She felt joy too for she knew that she was doing the
will of God and not her own will, and that she could help
You to better relations with Your children.

She said nothing of Joseph, but she must have thought
of him.

God's will was for him to be only a protector and
provider for her and the Child. She must remain a virgin.

But Joseph would be the happiest and most blessed
man on earth, because he would be as a father to the
Son of God.

She said to the angel, "Behold the handmaid of the
Lord, be it done to me according to thy word."

The Child was born and grew up to change the world
and to die on the cross.

She watched Him die in great sadness and in great joy
and triumph.

God's will had been done. The slaves of sin were freed.

The garden enclosed opened to all the world. She un-
sealed the fountain of peace and love.

Its splash and its spray refreshed and rejoiced and
remade the desolate, the beaten, the lost, the drug ad-
dict, the drunkard, the helpless, and all the brokenheart-
ed who had sought and found it.

My love for You, God, and for Your humble Maid of

Nazareth, now the glorious queen of heaven and earth, had a beginning. But please, don't ever let it end.

I know I could never love the Lady of the Trinity as much as You do, but I ask that You let me love her as long as You do.

Good night, God.

See You soon.

*And Elizabeth cried out, "Who am I that the Mother of my Lord should come to me?"*

I ask with the same wonder and rapture, "Who am I, Lord, that You and Your Mother come into my room and talk to me with tongues of fire?"

Who am I that I should lie here snug in bed, in pleasure or in pain, and talk to You with that same tongue of fire?

The light burns in a small red glass before the picture of Our Lady of Guadalupe. It licks the candle steadily, without pause, like the tongue of a little girl on a red lollipop.

Sometimes the tongue is silent.

Sometimes it reminds me of a woman sitting still and knitting something for her husband or her child.

Only her hands move; only her fingers and her needle. The needle flashes a rhythm of light, a code of love.

Sometimes the light is like a dancing girl, one who must leap and shiver and shake and make a thousand beautiful gestures to show her delight and adoration.

At other times, it makes me think of a kitten trying to juggle motes in the sunlight.

Sometimes when I wake in the dark of the night, I just say, "Hi," and go to sleep again, pleased and comforted like a child who wakes from a dream to see beloved faces bending over his crib.

At other times a fire speaks. It speaks of a Lady and her Son.

It speaks often of Our Lady's apparition to the Indian, Juan Diego, on the hill in Tepeyac in Mexico.

Sometimes it talks of the first time the maiden mother saw Her Son in the stable at Bethlehem.

"She was dressed in bright clothes when she first saw Jesus," the tongue of fire once said.

She was as bright and as glorious as the flame that talks to you. Her hair was fine and beautiful and long and red; red and gold; like the flame that speaks to you.

And she laughed like the little girl she was when the Baby played that trick on her.

One moment He was in her womb. The next moment He lay on the straw before her, smiling at her. Her laughter was so merry that even the worried Joseph laughed.

Never since the world began had anyone heard a laugh like that.

The virgin had given birth to a son, and she was still a virgin.

She knelt before Him. She touched His perfect little cheek. She caressed Him. She touched His perfect little hand. She kissed it.

She held Him close to her. She wrapped Him in swaddling clothes and placed Him in the manger.

Jesus and Mary found perfection reflected in each other's eyes, each looking into heaven.

Often I wonder how Juan Diego felt when he lifted his eyes on that hill in Mexico and saw his virgin Mother and heard her voice calling to him, "I am your loving Mother. I am the Mother of all your people. I want to help you and all those who love me and need me."

And I hear Our Lady using the pet name for Juan Diego, which we would translate as "Jacky Jim."

I lie in bed wondering how I myself would feel if suddenly I saw the Mother of God in her full splendor and heard her voice addressing me with love.

And often—how very often—I wonder how Jesus felt, both as God and as man, when He looked at the one perfect woman His Father ever created.

Jesus took more delight in her than did any of the saints.

The holier the beholder, the more rapturous the joy.

Only God Himself, Father, Son, and Holy Ghost, can really appreciate the power and the glory and the beauty and the wonder and the goodness of Our Immaculate Mother.

I suppose You were there too on that hill in Mexico where Juan Diego knelt at Our Lady's feet?

I suppose You enjoyed that same scene through all eternity, that You enjoy it now, that You will enjoy it forever and forever!

I suppose You gave Our Lady the power to imprint her portrait on the rough gunny sack of Juan Diego's tilma.

I suppose that's why there is a touch of eternity in that picture.

In four hundred years or more, the colors have not

faded. The material should have disintegrated naturally within a few short years, yet is still as good as new. The maguey fiber of which it is made has no stability in itself.

My tongue of fire has nothing of the Holy Ghost about it, nothing at all supernatural.

It is born of the scratch of a match.

But who am I to scratch a match and light a heaven on earth for myself?

Who am I to find out that anyone who looks at Mary looks at God? That anyone who sees a picture of Mary may see a picture of God?

Who am I to learn—at last—that the greatest delight of the children of men is to be with Mary and with her Father, her Spouse, and her Son?

*Lord, I thank You for Your gift of love I saw in a beautiful young woman's navel!*

She was dressed for the day in halter, shorts, and sandals.

The navel was where it should be, right in the middle of her slim, suntanned stomach.

It was a beautiful dimple, a delightful gem that only You could make.

Later that day I heard a woman whisper, just loud enough for me to overhear, "Wonder what he thought when he looked at that vulgar, air-cooled navel."

I thought how sensible this woman was to dress according to the day. How nice and cool and innocent she looked, a sight for angels and for men. (And also for other women of her age.)

I thought of men and women lying on beaches in various parts of the world, looking with love at Your water and Your sands and Your trees and Your serene blue skies and at You.

Looking at You and not seeing You at all.

Looking at each other, unaware that You were there.

When my brother Tom finishes his weekly letter, he signs it "Editor T."

When my brother Bill and other writers finish their copy, they sign it and they add a row of staggering X's. This is a symbol.

When a painter or an author or a composer finishes a work of art, he puts his name on it.

When a manufacturer has completed his product, he puts it in a container that bears his name. And maybe he stamps it—"Made in Japan," or "Made in America," or the name of the place where it was made.

The name or the initials or the symbols of these people mean, "completed—this is good—approved—grade A."

You, God the Creator, are the Great Artist.

You design bodies and souls. You design them in heaven and make them on earth.

Very often in these days vandals break into Your holy of holies, Your workshop, and ruthlessly destroy Your masterpieces.

But, if they permit You to finish Your work, You end it at the navel.

You sign it with a beautiful, divine, triumphant flourish of Your fingers. And You put a stamp on it which few of us can read.

"Made in Heaven for My glory on earth, and your eternal glory with Me."

We come not only from Your heart, but also from Your hands.

The navel is Your signature, Your divine O.K., Your guarantee of life for certain lengths of time, Your trademark, Your holy name written in the flesh.

The navel says, "This is a child of God destined for eternal life.

"This is a soul and body dear to Me.

"This is one of My potential saints."

It says, "This body is a work of Divine Love."

It says, "Little children, love one another."

It says, "Souls are born on earth and prepared to take over the kingdom of heaven when the right time comes."

Lord, You begin Your work by creating the soul.

The soul is the life, the spirit of the body.

The spark that starts the motor.

Without a soul there is no life, there is no growth.

Lord, what becomes of the souls who never have been given bodies?

What becomes of those who kill the bodies, and thwart the soul?

When I die, please, Lord, make that grand, triumphant flourish of Your fingers on my soul.

Give me a new navel for the old and put navels on the souls of all my readers and of all my enemies and friends.

Psalm 17

*Lord, Jesus Christ, Son of Mary and Son of God, You know that a pillow should not laugh, and that it should not cry.*

You were a pillow once to the head of Your beloved Saint John, so You know that pillows can love and pillows can mourn and pillows can pray and rejoice.

A pillow can bewail the departure of priests and nuns from convents and monasteries and rectories and far-off mission places.

It can feel heartbreak for these "shepherds in the mist" who, I think, are the loneliest men on earth, the most tormented, the most self-hated, and the most in need of You.

Be a pillow to them, Lord. Let them rest their sorry heads upon Your all-forgiving heart, and give them gentle sleep.

When a man rips off the Roman collar which is a symbol of the cross that bent the neck and shoulders of His Lord, he proclaims himself a free man.

So, willy-nilly, he has a cross for himself—and also a crown of thorns.

No man wears a heavier crown than his.

No man wears it in arrogance or pride.

The crown is never removed with pomp and ceremony, or polished and put away with solemnity and splendor for the next time it will be used.

These crowned heads indeed need pillows, pillows that do not laugh or titter.

No man who realizes he has been untrue to You feels he can be true to himself or true to the woman he may want to marry.

No man who denies You can do without You.

No man is a stranger to You, especially one who wears Your crown of thorns.

One who has loved You enough to give up all things for You doesn't leave You lightly.

He doesn't forget You easily, if he ever does forget You.

He doesn't truly live, without You.

You are closer to him in his wandering than You were at his ordination. You are in his conscience, as well as in his thoughts, in all his emotions, all his actions and ambitions and plots and plans.

You haunt him day and night.

You encompass him.

He has run away from You, only to find he has run into Your arms. (The same applies to the nun who breaks her vow of chastity, who leaves the convent and marries, or makes her own career in the world.)

Once You cried out on Your cross, "My God, My God, why have You forsaken Me?"

Isn't it true that all these stray sheep cry out, "My God, my God, why have I forsaken You?"

Perhaps, Lord, bearing this never-ending misery because he brought it on himself, the stray priest loves You more intensely than do some who never thought of fleeing from You.

He has crucified himself and dares not call on anyone to help him bear his pain. He feels it is right and just that he carry his cross alone.

The further he goes from You, the heavier it becomes.

He too needs a Simon.

Like all the rest of us, he is his own worst friend, and his own dearest enemy.

Every one of us falls into bad company—himself.

Priests are especially apt to fall into this bad company, because they are lonely.

They do not realize, always, that loneliness is one of Your best gifts. They do not realize what loneliness was Yours all Your life, especially that night in the Garden of Olives!

It does not occur to them that You would leave the agony of Your bloody tears to rush to them for what little human comfort they can give You but that You find them sound asleep.

They do not realize You wished to share Your divine loneliness with them in the same way You share Your divine love.

They do not consider loneliness as a token of Your love.

One must have someone he can talk to, someone who will understand him.

Sometimes he thinks that alcohol can be a friend who can help him through all his days and nights; sometimes

he thinks he needs a woman—a beautiful and understanding woman, perhaps a holy nun.

Priests are naive when it comes to women. They know
not what they do. Emotion often overbalances reason.

A Roman priest cannot serve God and wife. He is not
like other men; he never will be.

In Your own time, You will send the lonely priest the
violets and lilacs of Your grace.

I knew some of these anointed truants. I knew one in-
timately. We were in the same monastery when I was in
my early teens.

He was tall and strong and tender and funny and
eloquent and devout. I wanted to be like him.

Often, in the long summers, after a ball game, perhaps,
or some other form of recreation, a crowd of us would lie
in the shade of trees and wait for the ringing of the bell.

He would single me out for his pillow, lay his head on
my stomach or my chest and pretend to sleep. I would
laugh and he would scold me.

A pillow should never laugh, he maintained, or even
titter. It joggled the head that rested on it. It was made
only to give a tired man some comfort and peace and
honest sleep.

Lord, how I loved those days! How very white that
pillow was! And how many times, in less white years,
have I remembered a Man Who had no place whereon to
lay His head—and a pillow that had no divine head
resting on it!

How many times have I thought of Your Saint John!

The laughing pillow left the monastery a long time
ago.

The man who used the pillow in the shade of the trees
eventually became a priest.

He was a priest who loved You so very much that I
marvelled at him. He was a priest devoted passionately
to Your Mother.

In a violent fit of anger he walked out of the
monastery, forgetting both Your Mother and Yourself
and hurried as far away from the place as he could. And
there he met a woman who was young and beautiful and
as naive as himself. And within a week he married her.

I met him years later and hardly recognized him.

This was the "other Christ" who had rested on my hilarious, unbehaving stomach?

Impossible!

I was the nice white pillow he had liked so much?

Ridiculous!

Something happened then to both of us, something that led us both finally back to You, never to leave You again.

We found out that neither of us was free.

"The only job I could find," he told me, "was with the street car company. With the troubleshooters.

"One night when it was raining I was sent to fix a trolley line. I had rubber gloves on, but I knew that when I touched that wire I would die, suddenly, violently.

"I would be struck by God's most angry, most just vengeance.

"I said, 'All right, God, if that's the way You want it,' and I grasped the wire tightly.

"God didn't strike me dead, He struck me alive—that is, I began to live again and to love again."

He came back to You, Lord, the lost sheep coming back to the flock without Your having to go in search of him.

He brought his wife with him. The two became lay apostles in their parish and lived in poverty, chastity and obedience.

I saw him again, some months before he died.

"I'm happy now," he said, "that is, fairly happy. But oh if I could only say Mass once more before I die!"

I remember his hands on the wire and I thought of his hands on the Host.

He never said Mass again in a conventional way, but I think he said it in his heart continually every day of his shortened life.

Lord, when You strip the not-so-white pillow slip from my hard bumpy pillow, find me a place under the trees of heaven where I can laugh again as that priest pillows his head on my heart.

*We call You the Alpha and the Omega, God.*
And there is good reason why we should.
You are the Alphabet from A to Z and all the letters in between.
You taught us our alphabet but most of us never learned it properly. You gave us reason, but none of us reasons like others of Your children.
Men say, "We think therefore we are."
Other men say, "We are, therefore we think."
Only some of us think.
A child thinks You are a quarter with which he can buy an ice cream cone. When his father tells him that he could once buy five ice cream cones for a quarter, the child thinks, "God is getting stingy."
A beggar thinks God is a dollar bill that will give him a bite and a drink, and a bed in which he can sleep until they throw him out on the street at six o'clock next morning.
A politician thinks that God is a collection of five or ten dollar bills; one for the priest, one for each of the ministers in town, one for the rabbi and one for the new church that has just come into the district.
This not only insures votes, it also insures deductions from the income tax. And there is always a possibility that one of those clergymen is right and may be of some help.
To a banker or a broker, God is a million dollars and a few mortgages, and maybe a loan or two, and a tremendous building which will not only keep one's name alive for a hundred years but bless him with continual revenues every month.
To a Christian, God is love, abundance, security, eternity, heaven itself.
We use our reason to measure God.
God is punishment, we tell ourselves; therefore we say, "There is no God," or, "God is dead."
The poet says, "I need no God, I am a god myself. My mind is godlike. I too am a creator. Do I not create beauty in my own way?"
A musician says, "God is melody and music. God is song. I am a god."
The thief says, "Forgive me, God, I was tempted and I

stole it, help me steal some more."

The harlot says in her heart, "Forgive me, God, and help me."

A murderer says, "God help me, I didn't mean it. Have mercy on me, and don't let them find me."

We reason right.

We reason wrong.

We reason out justice to ourselves and others.

A bridge collapses and kills a hundred people.

A river rises and devastates a million acres of cities and towns. Famine kills ten thousand people in some faroff land. We call these acts of God.

A young girl feels a baby growing in her womb, but we do not call this an act of God.

In these days of easy morals and easy abortions we are not too concerned, we are provoked that God should invade the privacy of a young girl's life, but we know how to cancel His interference.

What right has God to go around giving babies to girls who do not want them?

Has a man no right to live his life as his reason directs him?

The Alpha and the Omega.

The A and the Z.

The A was there infinite ages before man learned to spell.

And the Z will be there long after the last man has finished his last lesson and the world has crumpled into dust and ashes or has evaporated in nauseous gases.

A B C D E F G ... every letter of the alphabet means I love You, God.

Do with me as You will.

Have mercy on the world.

Have mercy with all us unreasonable reasoners and bring us, all the good, the bad and the indifferent spellers, into heaven. Amen.

Psalm 19

*God, send us great men or we perish!*

It is not a time of greatness, so our need for great men is desperate.

It is an age of economic confusion, of strikes and picket lines, and hundreds of thousands of idle men.

And You know what flood tides of temptations come with idleness.

The average young American smokes too much, drinks too much, thinks too little.

He believes neither in heaven nor in hell, nor even in himself.

Many are thinking only of the million dollars they will make before they are twenty, in football, or hockey, or some other sport.

True, there are young people devoted to You and to Your Gospel, but there are not enough of them, and only You know how great they are.

Lord, replace the Kennedy brothers. Replace Martin Luther King. Replace Charles Lindbergh.

We killed the Kennedys, we killed Martin Luther King (and a crazy man killed his mother as she prayed and sang and played the organ music in her church for the Our Father. A beautiful way to die!)

We did not kill Lindbergh, but we kidnapped and killed his child.

Replace your great men, Lord, and protect them. Place Your grace about them so they may live many years.

We need them so.

We did not know how great the Kennedys were until we had killed them. And we knew because each changed the nation into a family of outraged and grieving brothers and sisters.

Give us great statesmen, great doctors and surgeons, great policemen, great military leaders (for we are in danger), great musicians, artists and writers.

Graciously answer Jack's inaugural prayer. Send us men who ask not what their country can do for them but what they can do for their country.

Thanks for Jim Bishop.

Dick Carroll and I and several others of his friends used to say, "That's our boy Jimmy," whenever he wrote something good. He is no longer a boy. He has become a full-grown man and he is on Your side.

He's a great writer. Protect him. Give him a long life.

Dear God, Our Father, do not abandon us, I implore You, though we have abandoned You.

Do not blot us out with the fire and brimstone of Your justice, as You destroyed the cities of Sodom and Gomorrah.

The people in America have grown cold in love and hot in lust; but we ask for mercy, not for justice.

We have washed Your name out of our schoolrooms as if it were a peril to young minds, as if it were a gross pollution that would destroy our little ones.

But we made no attempt to remove Your enemy from those schools, and many of the children have become barbarians who loot and destroy the classrooms, who sometimes attack the teachers, who burn down primary schools, and turn some high schools into bordellos.

There was a time, Lord, when Your name was passed from lip to lip in thanks and praise throughout all the Americas. Now Your name passes only from greasy thumb to greasy thumb.

It is written on our coins, "In God We Trust," but few people stop to read.

Some people think the word God is a misprint for "in gold we trust." But we do not trust in gold nor yet in silver. And gold does not trust us. Neither does silver.

Right now many of our people cry for justice, not for the poor, nor for the rich, not for the helpless nor exploited, but for Richard Nixon.

For him they want justice without mercy.

The righteous, the respectable, the distinguished—politicians, journalists, men of influence and might, wail like banshees against the pardon granted him by President Gerald Ford.

"Why him and no others?" they ask. "Have we one law for the powerful and rich and another for the poor and helpless?"

They are like so many lynch mobs crying, "Kill him—burn him—fill him full of lead—hang him—."

We have not changed too much since the days when men shouted, "Crucify Him, crucify Him . . . His blood be on our heads."

There were many widows in Israel in the time of drought and famine, but the prophet was sent to feed only one of them, "the widow of Sarepta near Sidon"; and there were many lepers in the land, but the healer was sent to only one of them, "a Syrian named Naaman."

We do not ask You, God, why You sent aid to only one of these widows and why You cured only one of these lepers.

If You told us why, we would not understand You.

I do not ask, "Why only Nixon?"

When we ask only justice for Nixon, true justice without mercy, we ask true justice for ourselves, true justice without mercy.

Forgive us, Lord, we know not what we do; we know not what we say.

True justice, justice without mercy, is found only in the fires of hell.

You visited Sodom and Gomorrah with Your justice and without mercy.

Abraham bargained with You for the lives of the people. You promised not to destroy the wicked cities if You could find five just men.

There are more than five just men in America, Lord. Maybe five thousand, maybe more.

I can name at least five for You beginning with Lincoln who had a dream of "government of the people, by the people, for the people," and a dream of "charity for all, malice toward none."

We shot him as we shot the Kennedys.

We shot the Kennedys, the President and his brother Bobby, because they had the same sort of dream.

And we shot the glorious dreamer, Martin Luther King.

Lincoln! The Kennedys! The Reverend King! And Lindbergh!

Do not abandon us, Lord; give us more men like Lincoln, like the Kennedys, like Martin Luther King, and like "Slim" Lindbergh.

"Slim" was a hero of the world, a demigod, an idol. I saw him flying to New York a day or two after his reception in Washington, D.C. His plane came circling, swooping over the harbor, shooting down.

Splash! Lindy!

The little boats splashed to him. The big boats raced to him. The whistles screamed. The whistles blew. There was a sound that never was by land or sea, before or since—a happy, hysterical, demoniac din. A thousand ships split their throats wide open to give him New York's warm welcome.

The world was made of water and ships and smoke and little flags, and noise and madmen.

There was nothing else but Lindy . . . his hair flying in the wind and the smoke, like the feathers of an eagle.

The greatest armada ever seen in the East accompanied him up the bay, screeching, honking, roaring, blowing off steam.

The smoke of a thousand smokestacks was in his eyes, and all the jumpy little flags of joy were there.

He was a knight in a blue-striped suit, a leather jacket, and a pair of goggles pushed up above his forehead. No king, no hero fresh from victory, was ever hugged so hard and so tenderly to the heart of the great city.

Mayor Jimmy Walker almost hugged him at the city hall. Nearly all the great men of the city would have liked to hug him. So would the hard-boiled cops who guarded him.

They took him up Fifth Avenue in an open car. And the glory-mad New Yorkers tore up ten thousand telephone books to give him a paper snow storm, the weirdest and most fantastic blizzard in the city's history.

Surely it took no less than ten thousand books to make that furious fandango of the paper snowflakes.

Bells rang. Whistles blew. Hundreds and hundreds of thousands cheered.

Women blew kisses or tried to deliver them in person. Women, women everywhere! Romance in every eye! And all the small boys crying his name, as they never cried the name of God.

Lindy! Lindy! Lindy!

Lindy was more than a hero. He was more than an idol.

He was a dreamer like Lincoln, like the Kennedys, like Martin Luther King.

He dreamed of peace on earth, good will to men.

I saw him standing at the foot of the Lincoln Monument in Washington two days before he flew to New York. President Coolidge and his wife were there with all the members of the cabinet and all the diplomats of the world, to do him honor.

A great parade had been arranged and he stood watching like a boy who has seen his toy soldiers come to life with gleaming bayonets and bright banners flapping in the wind, and listening to the martial music and the shouts and cheers of thousands and thousands and thousands of the people packed into Potomac Park.

He stood there slim and straight and humble, his hair combed only by the winds of heaven; and he spoke of peace on earth, good will to men.

The airplane he said had shrunk the world. It had made each nation a friend and neighbor of every other nation in the world.

I saw him place a wreath on the tomb of the Unknown Soldier and I marvelled at the contrast, the man who would never be known, and the man who would never be forgotten.

Splendid flesh and splendid clay!

Americans living and dead.

Send us more men like Lindbergh, Lord.

Send us more men like the Unknown Soldier.

Perhaps he too could be counted among the "just."

*Dear Trinity of all perfections, walking hand in hand with You, like a child with his father, I sang my song of the woods' siesta.*

It had no words.

Songs written by the heart are always silent.

But You heard and understood, and You blessed me.

The heart never had a tongue. If it ever learns to speak it will merely stammer or stutter. And it will repeat, forever, the only word it can learn.

That word is Love, or God.

Now I must put words to the song. For Your friends. For Your enemies. For those who do not know You. Much will be lost in the translation from heart to hand—for it is only with my hands I sing.

But if You help me, Lord, and if You sing the song for me, the world will know how much You love. And nothing will be lost.

It was a sultry day; yet it was cool in the forenoon, for there was a rowdy breeze.

I noticed it as we approached the bevy of young poplars. It was having fun. It had roused the grove into gales of leafy laughter that was so like the music of the brook that I mistook it for the brook—and wondered that the stream would sing so loudly on such a rainless day.

It was amusing to watch the hoodlum wind making the hoyden poplars believe he was a music master. He shook his long thin hair as he directed them. He waved his invisible baton like a mad chef mixing a tremendous salad.

He shook his incredibly thin arms. He danced. He capered. He turned somersaults. He spun himself in a hundred pinwheels.

The lordly firs and the dowager elms he annoyed, clownishly, rudely massaging them until they groaned and protested loudly.

He yanked at the cones in the pinnacles of the pines, as young boys sometimes yank at the pigtails of freckled little girls; and he jostled their top branches with his elbows, shrieking with laughter every time he said, "Excuse me."

He flattered and fluttered the fiddlehead ferns and the

grasses and weeds and shrubs in the ragged fields.

I don't know what nonsense he whispered, but they bowed prettily to him.

He did a wild adagio dance with the dust; he rippled the water of the stream; and he teased the shadows playing on the road, throwing fistfuls of light beams at them through the laughing leaves.

But gradually he tired of his sport, lost his energy, his zest, his will.

He yawned, he stretched, he curled up in a bed of poplar leaves and went to sleep.

I knew then it was the woods' siesta time.

The sky was cloudless, colorless, a clear wide window looking into heaven, and it was filled with the unbearable splendor of the sun.

It was noon.

The tall trees and the big rocks drew their shadows to them as the sun approached the hour.

These tough children of light had been playing on the road all morning, fighting the wind, fighting the intruding shadows of motor cars and dogs and men and women and of children on their way to school.

They are brats, these shadows, even though born of the sun.

They were only too glad to obey their mothers, to stand close to their sheltering skirts, for they hate and fear their awesome and brilliant father. They cannot bear his presence.

Little stones and pebbles on the road licked themselves clean and showed their good spots to the all-seeing eye of day.

Some glinted, making one think of ragged soldiers with medals on their skinny chests.

When the shining eye was no longer on them, the dull stones would go back to sleep, to drabness.

The ferns shook themselves free of some of the dust, as their lord passed over them. They preened themselves, even while bending low in that phony gesture of deep humility and profound respect they had learned so many thousands of years ago.

The poplars, unwontedly still and silent, had hoped to turn themselves into spangled and sequinned dancing girls, for the delight of the inspecting sultan. But the lazy wind wouldn't wake and help them. All they could show the monarch was the beauty of their green-gray satin leaves—and the lovely stains left on some by the lip-sticked mouth of Autumn.

Lord, why was Autumn here this summer day?

The poplars tried desperately to rouse the wind, but he merely turned restlessly in his dreams. The projected harem scene was a pitiful comic failure.

The pines threw their choicest cones in the path of their beloved, as Spanish windows sometimes shower roses on a serenading swain.

The road was filled with these exquisitely hard-covered seed cases of Yours, each entirely different from all the others, all as perfect as Your Spanish roses.

The oaks and the elms and the maples posed as great ladies.

The shrubs bowed stiffly, awkwardly.

A beautiful slender birch tossed kisses upward.

Only the brook kept working at the tasks You gave it, Lord.

It flashed a long bright smile at the sun, but it did not slacken its pace nor did it alter its song of praise.

The trees and the rocks went to sleep, the poplars snoring.

And, as soon as the sun had turned his back, his children, the impish shadows, sneaked around their mothers to play and to fight with other shadows on the road.

Only the stream stayed awake. A stream goes stagnant when it stops or sleeps. It dies of boredom, inaction, and green scum.

But even as it hurries through the land, the sun absorbs it, lifts it, holds it, fosters it—to let it down, eventually, as cool refreshing rain.

Of all the creatures in the woods, only the ever-working, ever-singing brook knows no siesta; of all the creatures in the woods, only the brook is invited to heaven by its lord, the sun!

A shabby, weary, bleary crow and a nasty little red squirrel broke the enchanted spell.

The bird, roosting high on an old white pine, leered

and sneered at me.

The squirrel jittered and jibbered and jeered. He was querulous, scurrilous, squirrelous.

(Lord, lift me from the quicksands of this silly mood that interrupts my song of the woods' siesta ... but not until I ask, "Why does a crow roost and a rooster crow?")

Lord, everybody besieges You all day and all night, asking for favors, begging for mercy, praising You, blessing You, adoring You.

I too.

No one needs mercy more than I.

No one so needs all the graces You offer.

But once in a while I have to tell You a joke or make some idiotic wise crack, hoping You will laugh.

I love to make happy those I love.

I think people can be happy if they laugh.

I know You have a sense of humor, for You created it.

I imagine You would laugh at us most of the time, if You were not so sorry for us and so concerned about us.

And if I feed You only the poorest corn when I dare to jest with You, it is because corn is all I have.

You did not spurn the widow's mite. You will not scorn my corn.

A black and white butterfly made me forget the intolerant squirrel and the too tolerant crow.

And a display of goldenrod made me forget the butterfly.

As I started to the goldenrod, I saw an exciting shade of red, low down beneath a blackberry vine. I thought it was a mushroom, but it was a strawberry leaf.

How often, how extremely often, Your strawberry leaves fool me in my hunt for mushrooms!

Yet, I am not vexed at this.

Suppose I had not seen the lively color of those leaves!

Suppose You had not blessed me with these eyes!

I picked the strawberry plant and studied it, standing a long time, a feast for deerflies and mosquitoes.

I considered, for a moment, the idea of gathering all the bright strawberry banners around and about me and making them into a garland for Our Lady.

You sang to me, God, as I held that three-leafed

strawberry glory in my fingers.

I do not know the words, if You used words. But it was about the tints and the mysteries in that trinity of leaves and the same tints and the mysteries in Your red-gold sunsets and Your gold-red dawns.

And there was something about other trinities.

There is a trinity of root and wood and bark; a trinity of plant and blossom and seed; a trinity of shape and smell and color; a trinity of soil and sun and rain.

There is a trinity of faith and hope and love in my heart and, in my mind, a trinity of intelligence and memory and free will.

Lord, swell my heart so it may contain enough love to spill out on all the world.

Whet my intelligence so it may always know Your will.

Strengthen my will so it may always do Your will and never mine alone.

Build my memory so it may not forget You, even for a second.

I listened in love and adoration while You sang; but the blue eyes of a wild aster brought me back to my song of the siesta—and the knowledge that impatient Autumn is knocking on the door of Summer.

And I saw the goldenrod again, a fresh clean spray. Beautiful beyond compare! And full of ants!

Lord, is it possible the insects believe this is real gold? How human can ants be?

Autumn is rushing up, the Autumn of the long day You have given me; some day my own siesta time will overtake me.

Lord, keep me working, like the brook, until that hour.

Keep me singing of Your mercy and Your love.

Keep me cheerful.

And when I close my eyes at last, no more to dream, let the world be filled with Your glory and with the radiance and the wonder and the perfume of Your mother . . . "the all holy, the immaculate, the most highly blessed, Our Glorious Lady."

Remember not the shadows of my sinful life.

Let there be no shadows when You come.

And, if You draw me to You, God, absorb me, hold me, bless me and let my songs, the murmur of a pitiful thin brook, fall gently down, like rain, into dry and shriveled hearts; into parched and thirsty minds; into wasted and barren souls; that they may be refreshed; that they may laugh and love; that they may bear You fruit.

# Psalm 21

*Dear God of Heaven and Earth, do You remember July 1st, 1958?*

Don't answer that, Lord. It is merely a rhetorical question for the benefit of those with whom You may share this letter. People like to know the date.

I was walking through Your woods, in Combermere, that morning. I had a long stick and with it I broke off the dead branches of the poplar trees.

I broke them off because they barred my way. The poplar starts branching when it is scarcely more than a twig. It has no mother to guide it.

When it grows a little it discovers it doesn't need the lower limbs. It lets them dry up and die. The mere touch of a stick will break them off.

"God," I said, "many dead branches bar my way to You. Break them. Break everything that keeps me from getting close to You—or You from coming close to me—as I beat a path through the poplar trees of my ears.

"Break off my attachments to earthly things, if they come between us. Peanut butter. Lobsters. Ripe cheeses. Hamburger sandwiches. Hot dogs with real English mustard. Bacon. Detective stories. Good books and movies. Comfortable shoes. Leisure. Fancy shirts and ties—donations, Lord, donations. And anything else.

"Smash all the dead wood in me, the branches I was so proud of in my youth and middle age, the twigs that shaped my life—and shut You out of it.

"Smash the live wood too, Lord, if it displeases You.

"Strip me of all my faults and let the dead lumber fall where it will—to be as forgotten as my sins."

I remembered a Russian peasant who had trained himself to think constantly of You and only of You. He walked from one shrine to another, saying, "God, God, God."

I envied him. He must have known a joy that approached the joy of Mary and Joseph. A heaven on earth!

But, I must wait, I think, for my heaven. I must wait Your time.

We were talking about this when the crows began to talk to You too and the grove became a chapel and a shrine.

I said to You: "I am a writer.

"I must think of other things besides You, in order to serve You—as I believe You want me to serve You.

"I must think of character, dialogue, motivation, plot, situation, mood, suspense, the right word in the right place.

"I must write books.

"Also I am one of Your Lay Apostles.

"I live with people, through people—and their generosity—and for people. I must think of people and their needs.

"I love You in my own way.

"I love You as much as my silly, sin-specked heart can love."

I watched the poplars and the pines adoring You, lifting their arms to You, whispering, "Holy, Holy, Holy!"

There were ponds of Our Lady's paintbrush everywhere, red and orange flowers. I watched them bowing and prostrating themselves before You.

They rippled with the excess of their love, singing Your praises silently.

They looked like pools of fire and their fragrance filled the world.

I saw the wild roses climb their vines to get a better look at You and Your Lady of the Trinity, our *Rosa Mystica*.

They hoped You might reach down and give them a friendly pat.

They blushed with their young love.

I saw the daisies, with the faces of happy nuns, blow ardent kisses to You as they curtsied in the winds.

I saw the buttercups lift to You their chalices of lacquered gold.

And I saw the humble, wild, white morning glories creeping forward through the sparkling dew. They came to touch Your blessed feet and to chant their Matins with their lovely pure throats, which You had shaped to the likeness of the old-fashioned phonograph horns.

Lord, in Your mercy, purge me unmercifully, so that when I too come to kneel at Your feet I may be as acceptable as those white flowers; and that I may have more to offer You than pale regrets.

A partridge shot out of the ferns and a flock of small brown warblers ascended with him. (Did I break up a prayer meeting of the birds?)

I thought of the partridge as a missile with the power and the speed of an Our Father exploding in Your heart.

I thought of the little birds as so many Hail Mary's and Glory Be's rushing up to You.

I put a prayer on every flower and every wing.

A simple prayer: "I love You."

I picked some of the wild strawberries You had placed on the hillside for me. They were fresh from Your hands, fragrant with Your divinity, sweet with Your breath.

My mother used to say, "God doubtless could have made a better berry, but God doubtless never did." I think it was a quotation.

She picked strawberries with me in Wisconsin, Lord, when I was a boy.

I picked them with the monks too, when I was studying to be a priest, more than half a century ago. What a wretched priest I would have made then!

God, tell my mother I thought of her in connection with wild strawberries—and with You. She'll like that.

The strawberry gives its sweetness joyfully.

The blackberry is a miser and a crab. He doesn't like to give. He surrounds himself with plenty of barbed wire.

But I'll dine on him just the same, come September.

There were plenty of blackberry vines at the shrine, Lord, and two beautiful big mushrooms. But the shyster worms had got there first and they had claimed the bodies. Ah well—worms have to be fed too!

My fingers were red with the juice of the strawberries. I licked them clean.

"O taste of the Lord and see that He is sweet."

Is that the way it goes? Not quite?

I thought of the Precious Blood of Your Son.

You are as generous with that Blood, Lord, as You are with Your berries. You have placed it everywhere for us, Your children, to sweeten our lives, to make us strong and holy.

You permitted it to dye the rocks in the Garden of Olives, the marble floors in Pilate's hall, the wood of the cross, and the soil of Calvary.

Yet it is still offered for us in half a million Masses every day throughout the world!

"O taste of the Blood of God and see that it is sweet!" (I offer my blood too. Such as it is, Lord, such as it is.)

Lord, why do Catholics have so many different versions of Your Word—and all of them far less majestic and moving than the language in the King James Bible?

We are confused.

"O taste and see that the Lord is sweet."

In the evening, in my room, I looked in *The New American Bible,* the Confraternity Edition. I also looked in the Gideon Bible I stole, years ago, from a hotel in Santa Barbara.

I found in both the words, "O taste and see that the Lord is good."

In the Catholic book these words followed: "Blessed is the man who flees to Him for safety." And in the other I found, "Blessed is the man that trusteth in Him."

Somehow, God, I think I would rather trust in You than flee to You for safety—though perhaps it comes to the same thing in a theological argument.

I hope I never have to flee to You for safety.

I want to stay in Your presence forever, even though I can never be like that Russian pilgrim thinking, "God, God, God!"

Lord, tell me something! Was I punishing myself symbolically—as the brain launderers put it—when I broke off the branches of the poplars?

Was I, unknown to myself, exhibiting a guilt complex that any psychiatrist would recognize at once?

Was I, in any sense, fleeing to You for safety—or fleeing from my "icky" self?

I don't know. I don't think so.

I was merely trying to get closer to You, God. You have been away from me so long!

There are times when You take some little one by the hand, lead him through green pastures, sit him beside still waters, and fill him with Your sweetness.

There are other times when You make him walk alone, without You, that he may learn to be a man.

Thank You, God, for letting me come close that day,

the feast of the Precious Blood.

Thank You for the sweetness of that hour with You.

Whether I walk alone again, or once more hand-in-hand with You, let me keep loving You.

Let me keep trying to come closer and closer to You.

I give You the confidence of Job, the confidence of a child.

"Though You slay me, yet will I trust in You."

Oh yes—and thank You for the full moon that night and the bracing coolness of the river.

And give my love to Mary and all my friends in Purgatory and Heaven.

*Dear God, Maker of all things, I thank You for this chill gray day.*

I didn't care much for it, at first; as You well know. It set a sad and somber mood in me.

I remembered Terry Ramsay's lead on the story of a funeral in Wisconsin: "Cloudrack of passing storm scattered cold drops of rain." His words made the tragedy bleak and grim and pitiless indeed—and taught me something of the ways of writing.

I remembered a night I spent at Laguna Beach with Wallace Smith, who kept waking every now and then to listen to the thunder of the surf and repeat again and again, "God's almighty fist!"

In his own way, Wally loved You too, Almighty God.

I think most honest newspapermen do love You, for they have a holy desire to make known the truth and a holy hate for Pharisees and phonies.

Do they not, somehow, remind You of Your Son?

Lord, I have many friends among American editors and reporters. I say this with the simplicity and something of the perfect trust of Mary when she let You know in Cana, "They have no wine."

You made wine for her.

You will show mercy to my friends, because You love me and because You love them too, more than I could ever love them.

Your gray rain brought back many memories.

Gray days have made shining marks in my long life. I thank You for them.

But it was not only memories the rain evoked.

It wakened me to the perfection of Your world, Your universe, Your power, and Your love.

I reflected that water goes up to You in mists from seas and lakes and ponds and rivers.

You use the sun to draw it into Your heaven. There You form it into clouds, which You tint with so much skill and magic that even the angels wonder at their beauty.

You send the clouds scudding before Your winds— each sailing off in the direction You have indicated —to bless some land below with rain or snow or sleet or hail.

We do not always see Your love in snow or sleet or hail or too much rain.

It is hard to see Your countenance in ice-stones that destroy a field of corn or wheat, yet we know You send us blessings even when we think we are accursed.

I saw the earth rejoice under Your gray rain today.

I saw young pines and spruces lift their heads a trifle higher toward You and stretch their limbs in gratitude and joy.

I saw the poplars shaking and shivering, like so many dogs emerging from the river.

I saw the wild strawberries scamper through the wet grass to show You the ripe, red fruit Your rain had brought them.

I saw the wild rose hedges in our garden light a thousand lovely pink and yellow fires to thank You for Your gift.

I saw wild flowers in the woods and hillsides tumbling out of their buds, so eager were they to see You passing.

I saw the river dimple with each gray drop that fell upon it and heard the wee creeks sing a loud Te Deum to You.

I saw the gold and gray and purple irises, and scarlet poppies and the cream-white lilies of the valley nod to You as they bathed and took new beauty on them.

I saw the daisies dance and sway and thought I heard them sing a hymn of benediction to You.

I saw the roads bedeck themselves in clean new Queen Anne's lace to give You honor.

I saw the devil's paintbrush bowing reverently to You and inhaled the powerful new perfume they offered.

The washed world smelled of paintbrush and of apples!

They call it after the devil here, because, they say, if you take it into the church and place it before an altar, it dies.

You know, God, it dies anyway after it's picked.

Some farmers don't like their fields painted by this orange-yellow blossom. It is a weed, they say, for when it dies it turns to a cottony sort of texture and flies all over the earth. It is, they say, a devilish pest.

To me it is most beautiful and its odor is better than

that of violets or roses. So I shall think of it hereafter as "Mary's paintbrush."

And may its aroma always remind You and her of my friends and me!

Before the rain had stopped and while the alleluias of the angels were still echoing across the heavens in a rumbling thunder, I realized that You use prayer the same as water.

Water lifted from the China Sea may sprinkle a garden in Ontario, or spoil a picnic in New York.

Prayers lifted out of Washington may soften and sweeten hearts in Vladivostok or Peking or prevent some crime in What Cheer, Iowa or Painted Post, New York.

Lord, is it strange such thoughts should come to me?

I do not think so, since they are born of love.

Is it strange that I should love You—I of all people?

No, it is natural, even for me, to love You.

But why must I show myself so blatantly, so imprudently, so extravagantly in love with You, Omnipotent Eternal God?

Others pay their court to You in solitude, in silence, in "gardens enclosed." They whisper their love and listen for the thunder of Your voice.

Why must I woo You in the glare of noon?

In the center of the world?

Why must I shout my love to You?

Why must I try to drown out the hucksters in the marketplace, the roar of traffic, the rumble of the subways and the "L" trains and the street cars and the screaming buses?

Why must I outshrill the policemen's whistle and the newsboy's "Read about it, read about it, Daily Paper, just out, read all about it"?

Why must I make my own raucous voice heard?

That someone, passerby or cop or vendor, may hear me plainly—and then may hear the silence of Your answer?

So be it!

Even from the first it was that way, was it not, My Lord?

Some readers thought me a sucker for selling my soul so cheaply. Some felt I was a saint.

I am neither saint nor sucker and it matters not, if

thinking of me leads them to think of You.

Was it a sucker bargain, God Almighty?

I gave You all of me and what did You give me in return?

All of Yourself!

If You wish it, I shall spend the rest of my life here.

"God's love for your love: God's love, going cheap: who'll buy God's love with his own?"

(I know I cheat You; and I know You love it.)

It is still new and strange to love You, God. The newness does not stale. The strangeness does not grow familiar.

The joy within me grows with the days.

Yet I remain the shallowest of vessels.

I share one species of infinity with You. I am infinitely shallow!

Strengthen my voice, Lord.

Give power to my writing.

Let every drop of mist climbing toward Your cloudy heavens remind You of my friends and me.

Keep raining Your graces, Your blessings, Your sovereign love into my shallowness as into a fountain that the divine downpour may overflow and splash the world with glory.

Psalm 23

*Dear God, Creator of the day and the night, for two or three weeks this little town of Winslow was the coldest spot in Arizona; perhaps it was the coldest area in all Your sunny Southwest!*

A doctor and many nurses had insisted on my coming here, so that I might walk in the desert sun every day. But there was snow on the ground, six or seven inches of it; and there was ice everywhere; and a man could break his backbone just strolling in the sunlight and the desert winds; and the sun was a sarcastic and mocking ball of frozen fire.

So it was wonderful when the sun thawed, and someone in this Arizona house suggested a ride toward Holbrook and the Painted Desert and the National Petrified Forest—"just a ride down the road and back, if only to enjoy the sun."

It was Sunday afternoon. There was little traffic on the road, and we filled ourselves with the beauty of the day.

White clouds came up from the earth, from the horizon all around us. Swan-white clouds. They rose majestically into the blue. I had never seen such a sky. I had never seen such a sky. I had never seen such dazzling clouds. The sun was high, and brilliant, and it made the clouds shine with Your glory.

My heart was opened wide to You, wide as the world around me. And I thought of the canticle the Dominicans say at Lauds:

"Ye angels of the Lord bless the Lord, ye heavens bless the Lord. . . . Ye fire and heat bless the Lord, ye cold and heat bless the Lord. . . . Ye ice and snows bless the Lord, ye light and darkness bless the Lord, ye lightnings and clouds bless the Lord. Let the earth bless the Lord, let it praise and exalt Him forever. Ye mountains and hills bless the Lord, all ye things that spring up on the earth bless the Lord."

There were feathers in those clouds. There were wings. And some, I thought, were not clouds at all, but the far-off tops of snow-covered mountains. There were mountains and ridges all around us, some near, some many many miles away.

The sun illuminated the clouds in the west, and

stroked them with sparrow-gray grease paint, here and there, to give them outline.

We went to Holbrook and came back. What was the Painted Desert to this panorama? You spread it out for us to see. It was a painted desert too. It was painted gray and white where the snow lay, and chocolate where the ridges showed themselves; and the road was a wide black streak in front of us and behind us. And the sun kept shining on the shining clouds. And my heart kept repeating, "all ye things that spring up on the earth, praise the Lord . . . All ye beasts and cattle, bless the Lord."

There were herds of cattle now and then, nosing a field of snow for such grass and shrubs as it might cover. Some stayed close to the fences where bales of hay had been set out for them. And, along one road, we saw a flock of antelopes saved from starvation by the conservation men.

"All ye beasts and cattle!" They were most certainly praising You that blessed Sunday.

"Life is a day," I kept repeating to myself, and to You. "Life is a beautiful day."

We arrived home in time to see the sun set.

If the day was so poignantly beautiful—and it was!—what can I say of the splendor of Your setting sun?

And what can I say about the blazing stars of Your night?

Lord, let this crazy heart of mine assume the size of the desert and of the sky, with all its wealth of pure white clouds, and its high blue dome; and let Your sun shine in it, and in every other heart, until the day is done.

*Dear God, Infinite Eternal Beauty, the sun is shining on a foot or more of snow.*

The world is made of powdered diamonds. The day is cold. A brisk breeze fondles the hair of Winter's long white beard; high above, a shepherd wind drives his shining flocks to new blue pastures.

The roads are open and sanded.

The evergreens drip with ermine and shimmer with sequins.

Other trees lift their whitened arms in protest (or in prayer) against the abandonment of Autumn.

Blue jays scream.

The river sparkles in the timid embrace of her lover, the ice. And hunters follow the tracks of dogs and deer.

I love, O Lord, the beauty of Your world and the land where Your glory hovers.

But I love much more the garden where Your Wisdom waits, which I have so recently discovered. I have just come from that oasis, Lord, and I think I know, at last, what St. Paul meant by looking "through a glass, darkly."

He was looking at You, wasn't he?

But it was like gazing at the midday sun. Had he looked with his naked eyes, he would have been blinded by Your divinity.

He saw You, not clearly, but enough to want to see You face to face.

I saw You through the same dark glass; but I saw You more clearly in this "garden enclosed" than anywhere else I have ever been.

I entered the gate like a tourist, led by St. Louis Marie de Montfort. When I left, I was reeling as though I had fallen off a merry-go-round, on which I had stayed too long.

I came close to reality there, God.

Is there anything more real than You, the Creator of all real things?

There is no snow in Your garden of Wisdom, no river flirting with new ice. There is no ice!

The flowers and trees are in bloom. The air is full of soft rich music and the murmur of heavenly voices. And there is an ecstasy beyond words—though it be expressed in words.

Wisdom! Your Word made flesh!

St. Louis tells me Wisdom is You, Almighty God.

All men are fools and only You are wise.

King Solomon was fool enough to trade his wisdom for a mess of women.

St. John spoke of Wisdom as though it were masculine. Solomon sang of it as though it were feminine—after the manner of men who love the things they know best.

This Wisdom was with You in the beginning, the king asserts; she was Your Craftsman, the maker of all the things that have been made.

His words were as soothing and sweet as the singing of meadowlarks, the humming of bees in a patch of clover, the rustling of coy winds in the fans of a palm grove.

"The Lord begot me, the firstborn of His ways, the forerunner of His prodigies of long ago; from of old I was poured forth, at the first, before the earth. When there were no depths I was brought forth, when there were no fountains or springs of water; before the mountains were settled into place, before the hills, I was brought forth; while as yet the fields were not made, nor the first clods of the world.

"Then was I beside Him as His Craftsman and I was His delight day by day, playing before Him all the while, playing on the surface of His earth, and I found delight in the sons of men . . . for he who finds me finds life, and wins favor from the Lord . . . .

"Come, eat of the food and drink of the wine I have mixed!"

As I read the words written by Solomon in all his glory, I heard the voice of Jesus echoing through the garden:

"For My flesh is meat indeed, and My blood is drink indeed. . . .

"Come unto Me, all you that labor and are heavily laden, and I will give you rest. . . . My yoke is sweet, My burden light."

St. Louis nudged me. "Solomon," he said, "refers to Wisdom as the mother and the artificer of all things. Note that he doesn't say Wisdom is merely the source of all things. He notices that Wisdom is also the mother of them—a mother loves what she has made."

I went back to the words of Solomon, reveling not only in the majestic poetry in them, but also in the new meanings I found there.

"I pleaded and the spirit of Wisdom came to me.

"I preferred her to scepter and throne and deemed riches nothing in comparison with her.... All gold in view of her is a little sand....

"Beyond health and comeliness I love her and I chose to have her rather than the light, because the splendor of her never yields to sleep.

"Yet all good things together came to me in her company and countless riches at her hands; and I rejoiced in them all, because Wisdom is their leader, though I had not known she is the mother of these."

I read on and on—"Such things as are secret I learned and such as are plain, for Wisdom, the artificer of all, taught me ... she is an aura of the might of God and a pure effusion of the glory of the Almighty.

"Therefore naught that is sullied enters into her.

"For she is the refulgence of Eternal Light, the spotless mirror of the power of God, the image of His goodness, and she, who is one, can do all things....

"Passing into holy souls from age to age, she produces friends of God and prophets....

"She is fairer than the sun and surpasses every constellation of the stars.

"Compared to light she takes precedence ... she reaches from end to end and governs all things well."

How often old Solomon speaks of light!

How often do I remember that Jesus was the Light to enlighten the gentiles?

"I am the Light of the world."

"From the mouth of the Most High I came forth and mistlike, covered the earth.

"In the highest heavens did I dwell, my throne on a pillar of cloud. The vault of heaven I compassed alone, through the deep abyss I wandered.

"Over waves of the sea, over the land, over every people and nation I held sway. In all these I sought a resting place; in whose inheritance should I abide? Before all ages, in the beginning, He created me and through all ages I shall not cease to be.

"Like a cedar on Lebanon I am raised aloft, like a cypress on Mount Hermon, like a palm tree in En-gaddi, like a rose bush in Jericho, like a fair olive tree in the field, like a plane tree growing near the water.

"Like cinnamon or fragrant balm or precious myrrh, I give forth perfume.

"Come to me all you that yearn for me and be filled with my fruits; you will remember me as sweeter than honey, better to have than the honeycomb.

"He who hungers for me will hunger still, and he who drinks of me will thirst for more. . . ."

"But," I heard the voice of Jesus, "he who eateth My flesh and drinketh My blood hath everlasting life and I will raise him up in that last day . . . he that eateth Me, the same also shall live by Me."

I reread the lines, "Like a cedar of Lebanon . . . like a cypress on Mount Hermon" . . . and I began to understand why these words are sometimes used to commemorate feasts of Our Lady.

She is the Seat of Wisdom. She is the mother of Wisdom. And she was with God "in the beginning."

And I found a *story* in Your garden, Lord! One of the greatest stories in all history.

A newspaperman, I suppose, is never content with learning new truths; he has to have a story as well. A new story.

A story worth the writing.

This is the story of man's fall in the garden of Eden and Your Wisdom's solution of an impossible situation.

Man had sinned against His Creator, against divinity.

He could not possibly atone, since he was merely human.

Infinite Justice demanded he be punished as Lucifer had been punished.

Infinite Love—equally powerful—insisted he be redeemed.

You had a tender spot for us sinners even then, Lord.

The first proof of this was what You did for Adam and Eve when You saw them shivering and shamed in their fig leaves.

You, their Almighty and Indignant God, made them

"garments of skin"!
You clothed them decently!
You made them comfortable!
So Your justice was arrayed against Your Love, or Mercy.
How was this awful contest to be resolved?
It was easy for Your Wisdom.
Man could not atone adequately unless he were divine?
Then Wisdom would find a spotless virgin and through her, become a man. Being both Your justice and Your love!
God, what tremendous stories are still hidden from me in Your sacred books?
As I was about to leave the garden, St. Louis spoke to me of Mary. "She is," he said, "the secret magnet that draws Incarnate Wisdom so powerfully He cannot resist.
"This magnet drew Him down to earth. It will draw Him every day to every man.
"To possess Eternal Wisdom, we must possess His mother, Mary. She will help us keep Him.
"I ask you, what would it benefit us to acquire Divine Wisdom, if, like Solomon, we are so unfortunate as to lose Him again?
"Let us not trust in ourselves.
"Let us trust in Mary. And let us consecrate ourselves to Jesus, the Incarnate Wisdom, through the hands of Mary."
Lord, let me keep such little wisdom as I have; and at the same time, let me stay Your fool.

Psalm 25

*Dear God, Eternal giver of eternal life, a long time ago*
*Your poet, Henry Longfellow, wrote the famous line "A*
*boy's will is the wind's will, and the thoughts of youth*
*are long, long thoughts."* Please tell him he is one of my
favorite writers. It must be a long, long time since he
received any fan mail. Even in heaven a writer needs a
kindly word now and then.

It is true my will shifted often, like the wind, when I
was growing up. But the prevailing winds were right off
the press, and they steered me, forcefully, and inevitably,
into the whirlpool of the life of a newspaperman. My
father wanted me to learn some craft or trade. But no
trade winds blew my way. Not ever.

Indeed my thoughts were long, long thoughts. Yet,
Lord, my thoughts now are longer than those of any boy.
They do not leap ahead, as they used to. But how long
they stretch back, into my lovely fresh-green spring!

Lately I think of the newspapermen I knew and envied
and admired and loved. Thank You, Lord, for keeping
me out of all high schools and colleges, and sending me
to the university of life, where all the teachers were
newspaper men and women.

My wife, Mildred, who had been a newspaperwoman,
used to say, especially at parties, that she pitied the
wives of newspapermen.

She was sorry for them because they could never tame
their husbands, remake them, or change them into ordinary men. They could not even keep them at home. If a
good story broke anywhere within a hundred—or perhaps even a thousand—miles, the husband was sure to
be sent there. And he was likely to stay a week or more,
having a good time writing stories for his paper. He
loved to write, but he never wrote his wife. A woman was
crazy to marry a newspaperman. She should marry a
grocer or butcher or tobacconist or druggist, and live up
over the store. Then she would always know where her
husband was, and what he was doing.

She would pause a moment, and then say, in that
mournful way she could adopt whenever she wanted,
"There is only one type of woman I pity more."

Someone was sure to ask, "What type is that?"

Mildred always answered: "The woman who does *not*

marry a newspaperman."

We both knew that newspapermen were the salt of the earth; the only free men on this earth; the only men who really loved all the things on this earth. They didn't work for money. Not exactly. They liked money, of course, and always wanted more. But they would work for nothing, if they could afford it. They worked for the love of working. They had no union hours in those days. It was nothing to work twenty-four hours on a story. Once I went without sleep for forty hours—at the mouth of a mine where twenty-four men were trapped—waiting for news I could put on the wire. Any moment that news might come up from below. The men had been found! They were alive! They were dead! Some were alive! I had to be there and awake, when the story broke.

Newspapermen were as dedicated as priests and nuns to their jobs. And they were more loyal to their papers than to their friends or their wives or their own welfare—more loyal, usually, than the papers were to them.

They were all different, these men. Different in every way. Each was a distinct individual. There were no carbon copies. Yet they were all the same in some ways. They were wise. They were wily. They were generous and genial. They were always willing to help another newspaperman—while eager to cut his throat over a story. When it came to scooping the reporters of rival papers they were merciless. Still, often, they would write a story for a pal who had fallen a little drunk on a big yarn, and who would certainly lose his job if he didn't deliver. It was almost as bad to lose a good newspaper job as it was to lose a wife.

They were hard-boiled realists. They were sentimentalists. They were honest and hard-working seekers of the truth. They were undaunted, intrepid, valiant, unconquerable. They always got the story, no matter who said no. Fight city hall? They did it every day. Nobody bossed them. Nobody fooled them. Nobody bribed them. Nobody overawed or frightened them. Against all odds they found out the truth and put it in the paper. And how proud, how very proud, they were, to be what they were!

They were witty and gay. They had many talents. They were artists, musicians, athletes, philosophers, critics, psychiatrists—before psychiatry was born. I knew one who opened a wall safe in the home of a burglar. He opened it because the burglar politely asked him to. The burglar had forgotten the combination. This same reporter once went to the organ in a home where we were spending the night—we were working on a story in Utah—and played such music that everybody but me cried. I think I was busy writing a story to be taken to the nearest telegraph office by a Mormon cowboy and put on the wire for the Chicago Tribune. We were hunting "Old Chief Posey" at the time, a Paiute Indian wanted for murder.

They were skeptics all, wary men, readers of hearts as well as minds, always on the watch for hidden motives, always alert for a weakness or a fault—or a wound that would let out the imprisoned truth. But when they gave their friendship to a man, it was for life.

I loved those men. I still love them, though most of them are in Your keeping now—and, I trust, happy to be numbered among Your staff. I love these men who work for You and give You everything they have and ask for nothing in return.

There are no happier men anywhere on earth.

A boy's will is the wind's will, but my will is strictly Yours.

*Dear God, Lord of all beauty, this August day is one of the loveliest You have given us.* It is almost ninety in the sun, but there is a gentle breeze to temper the heat. And there are clouds in the oyster-shell sky, which promises cool showers. Your roses are still with us, red and yellow and pink and white. It is strange to see so many roses so late in the summer. Their aroma is like a prayer of thanks.

In the gardens there is a wider variety of colors than one could find in the plaids at a Scottish picnic. The dahlias are at their best, and have grown tall enough to look over the heads of the gladioli so they can watch the people passing and the statue of St. Joseph in his niche. The nasturtiums are massed against the petunias— bright gold against a thousand shades of royal purples. And the marigolds are keeping company with the bachelor buttons.

The pansies are running all around the borders of the garden; and they are not looking at St. Joseph at all, at all. They're too busy calling attention to themselves. They're too busy making faces at each other.

Someone is mowing the lawn with a power mower. The clean sweet smell of grass adds itself to the fragrance of the garden, and the sound of the motor is pleasant. God, would You quit loving me—just like that—if I said I like the moaning sound of the motor? You just couldn't quit loving me, nor any other man! No matter what I did, or what they do!

The apple trees are heavy with fruit. The apples will ripen in a few short weeks. They are as pretty as the flowers. Some other trees, envious, perhaps, of the orchard, are showing flashes of color. And, in the woods, tall maples are wearing red and orange pennons on their lances.

Mushrooms are so plentiful this year a man gets tired picking them up and carrying them home. They stand up boldly in the pathways and in the shelter of little pine trees, tall ferns, and monstrous blackberry canes. And most of them, Lord, are perfect. Many thanks!

But the most beautiful thing in this part of the world, to me, is the statue of Our Lady of Sorrows, which stands in the orchard.

There is something symbolic in this, maybe. For, in our happy-go-daffy way, we have turned the tree of the Knowledge of Good and Evil—the forbidden tree in the Garden of Eden—into a sour apple tree. And we have blamed Eve and the apple for all the trouble we must suffer.

One seeing the statue of Our Sorrowful Mother among the apple trees naturally thinks of Eve and naturally wonders what Mary is doing in that particular place.

It is not hard, Lord, to envision Our Lady standing in a crowd of people instead of in this orchard, and to see no birds flying over her, to hear no bees buzzing around her; only to see and hear a jeering, yowling, hissing, spitting mob of sinners!

It is not hard to imagine her standing before a cross, not as a statue but as a living woman; and to imagine the cross not just a symbol but the beams on which her son was crucified. It is not hard to think of Jesus hanging on that cross, making love to men as He dies . . . making love to men who hate Him!

You put words in my mind, God, which seem to be in the heart of Our Lady!

"A river rose in Eden, watering the garden; and from there it separated into four branches. I see three rivers here, flowing out of this new Eden, three red rivers. One flows from His right hand. One flows from His left. One flows from His two feet nailed together.

"I see three rivers watering the garden of the world, irrigating its arid soil, making it bloom, making it fruit-ful, making it beautiful and holy.

"I see three rivers springing from the Body of God, carrying cargoes of grace, freight rich enough to redeem every slave that Satan has in his keeping.

"But where is the fourth river?"

A Roman lance is thrust into her Son's side, and the fourth river pours itself out into the waiting world.

"Four rivers," Our Lady says. "Four rivers flowing out of Eden, bearing the greatest treasure of Almighty God! Four rivers that will bring even the weariest sailors quickly back to the Paradise they seek! Rivers of God's most precious blood! May they flood the world with mercy!"

Psalm 27

*Father in Heaven, we said the Rosary last night in the beauty of Your long summer twilight, on the front lawn.* And, as usual, Lord, I was distracted during prayer. Yet, at the same time, I was conscious of Your presence.

The birds were in the trees at the river bank. Robins and purple grackles and swallows and a few poor sparrows. They twittered and chirped as we prayed. And now and then they went soaring upward, like our prayers. I remembered You in the birds, in their song, their swift flight, their varied colors. And I remembered Your Son and His words about the sparrow.

I looked at the dim clouds to the south, far away white clouds that looked like a collection of soft gray veils. They turned the sky from a deep azure to the shade we know as "baby blue." And I saw You there in the clouds, moving them a little, as though to get a better look at us assembled on the grass of the lawn.

There was a slight breeze, and it rumpled the water of the lovely river, close to the nearby sands. But farther off, toward the shore near the church hall, the water was still and dark and solid. You held it still, so that I could see the hall and the trees reflected in it. The tall white birches preening by the river bank, growing taller each year, went far into the depths of that mirrorlike water. I thought of Your Son who once walked upon the water. Thus, I saw You on the surface of the magic river, and in the trees and the clouds above it, and in the depths below it where the reflections of the tall white birches stretched themselves luxuriantly and lazily.

You were in the breeze that stirred the young bud-leaves of the red maple, and the fresh and pungent foliage in the clump of cedars, and that ruffled the water near the shore. And it seemed to me that with the breeze, You were joining us in the praises of Your Mother: "Blessed art thou amongst women and blessed is the fruit of thy womb, Jesus."

I tried to picture Jesus in the Garden of Olives. I tried to picture His agony. But my mind wandered, like the wind. My mind is a wind, Lord; and hard to keep blowing in any one direction very long.

I remembered the delight You gave me on that early May day when I went for a short walk in the woods. I was tired that day, and could not have walked much farther. So You let me see them right away. Those beautiful yellow blossoms. I picked them and brought them home. I didn't know what they were. I only knew You had given them birth and their beauty of scent and shape and color.

"Dogtooth violets," someone cried out when she saw them. "Also known as adder's-tongues!" She was as delighted as a little girl who sees the first ice cream man of the summer. I felt like the man in my friend Louie Davidson's story, who in his middle forties decided to be educated, and thus learned to his astonishment and added self-pride that, though he did not know it, he had been speaking prose all his life. I had been picking those yellow posies every spring for the last twelve years or so and had never even tried to find out their name or species. All these years I had gathered the first dogtooth violets of Your spring! I had seen You in them. And I guess it didn't matter what they were called. By any other name they would still have spoken to me of You.

I saw the wind tease the still water and rub out all the reflections; and I remembered the rapids of a certain river.

We were not looking for rapids. We were looking for caves. We were out for a drive, and we had seen signs, with arrows pointing this way and that, advertising the caves.

We asked directions, but nobody knew exactly where the caves were, nor how to get there, though most of those we asked had lived in this small town all their lives. Eventually we saw a sign and a pointing arrow. We followed the road a long way. It branched off here and there. There were no signs. And nobody knew whether we were headed in the right or wrong direction.

Life is like that too, God. Sometimes we do not know the right road to You. And even those who live close to You do not seem to know exactly how we can reach You. What is that old motto—"The closer to the church, the farther from God"? Maybe there's something in that, but I hope not; for my room is separated from the chapel only by a corridor and a tiny bedroom.

We had gone several miles without seeing any signs,

without meeting any natives. Then, as we were about to cross a bridge, we saw two little girls.

"The Caves?" the older one said. "Oh, them!"

She seemed, somehow, disappointed in us. What, in the name of common sense, did two grown up men expect to find in this part of the world, two men in a fine automobile like that? Mere caves?

"Them," I said. "Are we anywhere near them?"

"Oh, them!" the child said once more. "Just over the bridge. But they're locked up today. The man that owns them is away. They ain't so much anyway. You go in one and out another. And what do you see? Just caves."

We didn't go through the caves, Lord, but we did explore the grounds; and we peeked into one cave entrance that had a gate on it, and a padlock on the gate.

But I spent most of the time just looking at the rapids in the river.

I fancied myself as the narrow river bed into which all this water flung itself so musically, so joyously, so forcefully, so wholeheartedly. You had just fed the stream with the last of Your snows, and the current was swift and full. And I likened it to Your love.

I watched this torrent of Your love pour itself into that narrow channel, and the colors it made in those little falls. In some places the water was black or dark blue. Just above the rocks it turned into a rich rusty wine like that used in the Mass. In the sun, the rapids had all the rainbow's glory. And in the white swirling lace among the rocks I fancied I could see, now and then, the swift glimpse of an angel's wing.

A long, long time I stayed there staring, Lord. I said to myself: "I am like this narrow channel into which Almighty God so violently sends the overwhelming tumult of His love. He flings Himself against me, but I resist Him, like those rocks resist the water." I asked You, God, to smash the resisting forces in me and wash them away so that I might be filled with You, might no longer be part rock, part stream; part me, part You; might be entirely You. But then I thought of something else.

That flood of water battering the staunch rocks could be the temptations of the world trying to occupy the whole channel of my being. In that case, Lord, I wanted the rocks to remain strong; and to keep resisting until the end of time—the end of breath for me.

I made a fumbling effort to meditate properly on the last decade; but there is little concentration in me, and I drifted back to the rapids.

I was, I decided, neither rock nor river, but merely the froth born of their conflict—"less than the scum beneath Thy heavenly feet"—yet I wanted to be a mighty torrent of fresh water rushing through a God-thirsty world, singing of Your love and Your beauty and Your mercy and Your almighty power. Forgive me, Lord, for the fool I am, and help me to be less frothy.

*Dear God of Every Day and Every Hour, I ask a special favor of You.*

It is a simple request, Lord, though it may make You smile, as a Father sometimes smiles upon a stupid child. Let me never be bored by Your miracles! That is what I ask of You, for this anniversary present. Let me never yawn at any of Your wonders!

Never let me take You for granted, as I am prone to do.

Let me enjoy the miracle of waking, when it comes to me, and the miracle of being aware that I am still alive, a breathing, walking, thinking miracle of Your love and mercy. It is a miracle that You made me, Lord. It is a greater miracle that You tolerate me. And that You love me—Lord, God, I cannot even begin to comprehend the immensity of this marvel!

I am a miracle, for You made me and put me here. Yet I dare complain, sometimes, that I do not feel as young as I was yesterday, not as willing, nor as able. Let me not slight this miracle of Yours, Lord, nor the miracles I see every day around me. So many, many miracles! So many beautiful miracles!

Let me see Your image clearly in the people around me, these people who have given you the warmth and wealth of their youth. You work miracles of grace in them every day.

Let me not take them for granted, Lord; let me never be bored with them. Let me not be bored by anyone; for every man and every woman and every child on earth is a miracle of Yours.

Let me not take Your seasons for granted. Spring is a miracle. Summer is a miracle. Autumn is a miracle. And winter is a beautiful miracle and it lasts a long long time, here, Lord, a very long long time. Every new day is a miracle, and so is every night.

Food is a miracle. Clothing is a miracle. Houses are miracles too, since You gave man the brains to build them. Health is a miracle. And so, I think, is sickness. Not all the time, Lord, but frequently, sickness is a miracle of grace, because it brings the patient a closer image of Your face, a better understanding of Your love and care, a more intimate relationship to You.

And death, of course, is the greatest miracle of all, for it is both birth and death, and it blots out all the things that come between us, Lord, between the likes of You, that is, and the likes of us. It blots out everything, and brings us face to face!

God, shall I be able to stand it, when I see You thus? If Our Lady is with me, yes. If she isn't—God have mercy on me!

Laughter is a miracle, Lord, that we do not appreciate as we should. And there is much laughter here. The other day a white cat climbed up a tall pine tree, perhaps tempted to the heights by wicked blue jays. But he was too frightened to come down. A young boy climbed up for him.

"Nothing wrong with him," the lad reported. "He just thought he was a pussy willow."

Thank You, Lord. Thank You for all men and women. Thank You for birth and waking and sleep. Thank You for leisure and work. Thank You for sickness and for health.

Thank You for the beauty of this region, Lord. For the river. For the woods, and the berries and the mushrooms and the wild apples and plums and the millions of flowers that grow miraculously there. Thank You for the many lakes and hills. Thank You for the changing seasons, for rain and frost and snow and brilliant sunshine. Thank You for sunrise and for sunset. Thank You for the moon and the stars. Thank You for the birds that flit all around us, even if they do awaken us at 5:00 A.M. or sooner. Thank You for the visitors who come to see us, and for their generosity to us, and their tender friendship.

Give me this present, Lord, the gift of appreciating You and all You do. Someday I will ask You for the gift supreme, that I may love You as I should . . . and more than yesterday . . . and less than tomorrow.

Psalm 29

*Dear God, Maker and Giver of all things, let me start this new year, this new decade, praising and thanking You.*

Let me live it, or such part of it as may be left in the stockpile of my days, in the awareness of Your presence, in the knowledge of Your constant love and in an ever-increasing love of You.

I have treated You most shamefully.

Let me make up to You, somehow, for my neglect.

I didn't realize my rudeness, my ingratitude, my forgetfulness until You took us to that strange new restaurant, the day my friend Gene passed the doctor's examinations.

I thought, at the time, that we had found the place by ourselves.

Now I know You directed us to it.

It was Saturday evening and the home town had won a tremendous football victory. The city danced with liquid jubilee.

The place was crowded. Gene and I stood outside in its doorway for some little time, not quite certain we wanted to go in. We wanted a fairly decent dinner, something with which to celebrate his new lease on life. If we couldn't find room inside, we would mosey on.

Just as we were getting ready to leave, a Good Samaritan waved to us from inside and made us welcome.

"I'm having some trouble," he confided in us. He smiled as if we were old friends, as if we could understand and sympathize. "Too many waiters are football fans. They didn't show up. There are plenty of tables still vacant, though, and if you don't mind waiting . . . ?"

He was a warm, charitable, hospitable man. He seemed sincere. So we said we'd stay and wait. He thought that was wonderful of us, and he sent some cocktails to our table: "On the house."

Some of the glow faded when we looked at the prices on the menu. We wanted to get up and go. But charity trapped us, held us. We could not be discourteous.

There was but one thing to do. That was to order the "specialty," which seemed to be the only bargain on the printed bill of fare.

It would have been a bargain at any price, for it brought You close to me, Lord.

"Relax," Gene said. "It seems to me Our Lord and Our Lady brought us here. They must have had some good reason. We have enough money. We have plenty of time. And we have something to celebrate, just like these football fans.

"God wants us to enjoy this."

It was a sort of nightclub. The tables were close to each other. We could hear what everybody around us was saying.

They were most young. They looked prosperous and happy. They were loud and gay. They drank more than they ate. Their drinks were of all colors.

There was a jazz orchestra and a blonde singer with a pleasant voice.

We sipped and waited and ordered. Hors d'oeuvre Riche. Consomme au sherry. Feuilleté de champignons à crème. Filet mignon Pompadour. Pomme de Terre Noisette. Fonds d'artichauts étuvés au beurre. (Your friends, God, might like to know what we ate.)

Lord, You know we have some wonderful cooks at home. You also know that we seldom eat anything rich or expensive.

You know how we act when we are invited to a restaurant or to someone's house.

You know how I felt about those hors d'oeuvre, for instance—particularly the anchovies, those little garlands of fish and brine and oil, those lovely dark curved morsels that put such bitter salt joy in one's mouth when his teeth abrade them.

You know my stand in regard to mushrooms and filet mignon and wine in my soup. (I am for it!)

The atmosphere of the place changed with the coming of the hors d'oeuvre. It was almost like being in a cathedral.

I became aware of You.

I became aware that I love You, and conscious that You had always loved me, even when I was far away from You.

Strange!

The man with his back to us, who kept ordering a double rye with ginger ale every few minutes, talked to himself aloud.

He had won $100 on the game and was going to drink it all down. He was a great man, a strong man. He had been a wrestler. He was a $12,000-a-year man.

The government tax collectors were stealing him blind. He was alone. He liked it that way. "Waiter, another double rye—where the hell is that waiter?"

The thin young man on our left introduced his girl to everybody. "Mr. Horwitz, I am very proud and happy to present my future wife, Anna." One man said, "Anna! The closer to the family the further from formality! May you be happy always, Anna."

The singer sang. The musicians played. The diners dined and sipped and talked and shouted and flirted. I heard and saw everything and everyone.

I was absorbed in talking to You, God, yet aware of all that was happening around me.

I became aware too that this was not the first extraordinary dinner You had arranged for me.

On the contrary!

I realized, for the first time, that You had been feeding me all my life; even when my nourishment was but the rich warm milk of my mother.

Day after day, wherever I was, whatever I had done, You had attended me, watched over me, provided for me.

No matter whether I was good or bad, You loved me!

Your Son taught us to pray to You: "Our Father Who art in heaven."

You had been a Father to me—and what scant attention I had paid to You!

Often I had said grace before and after meals. But usually I said the words mechanically; with no more fervor than a busy man dictating letters. "Dear sir . . . in regard to yours of the 19th, beg to say the shipment was gratefully received and in reply would state . . . yours very sincerely."

Until this moment I had never been quite conscious that You were the Host at every meal.

The Host and also the Guest of Honor!

I had never really thanked You.

Yet it had made no difference to You, apparently, for You kept showering me with Your love.

How amazing that You love us, God!

And how tragic that so few of us have any idea of Your love for us!

Most of us were brought up in the belief that You are a miser, a tyrant, a God of anger and jealousy and vengeance, a greedy Deity Who wants everything we have and Who will send us to hell if we hold back anything at all.

You are pictured as Infinite Selfishness, when all You want for Yourself is our poor human love!

In that overcrowded hoyden nightclub restaurant, surrounded by people seeking to be happy, I tried to make up to You—with a few minutes of pure love—for the long, long lifetime of rudeness and neglect and ingratitude and sin!

But I need more time, Lord. I need all the rest of my life.

I gave You only a few minutes, against a lifetime of Your unceasing love and care!

The odds are still with You, God.

They always will be.

It was not only in the matter of food and drink that You showed Your love to me.

In those few moments I remembered other things.

I remembered the morning in Sudbury, Ontario, when I got up late and went looking for a nine o'clock Mass. I went to the "French Church" first. But a funeral was entering the front door. There would be a Mass of Requiem, and probably I would not have a chance to go to Communion.

I went next door to the "English Church."

(Why do You have two Catholic churches in the same block, God? Don't people know You speak and understand both languages?)

In Christ the King Church the altar was decorated for a Nuptial Mass. I decided to wait.

I listened to the bells: the joyful bells ringing for the wedding, the sad bells tolling for the death of one of Your children.

I thought of the women You gave me, Lord. The

beautiful, loving, brilliant women. The extraordinary
women.

I have thanked You many times for each of them—but never enough.

I have been blessed beyond all other men I know, in the love and devotion of the women You gave me.

I thought too of the woman You chose to be Your mother, the loveliest of all the lovely women You ever made, and of her wedding to a humble carpenter.

I thought—a little—of the death You have reserved for me, the last bride in Your giving.

What will she be like?

It does not matter, I thought, so long as she comes from You.

There was a general Communion at the Nuptial Mass. Nearly everybody went to the altar rail. And You fed us with Yourself!

I felt very close to You, God, dining on filet mignon and mushrooms and an artichoke heart or two.

How is it that I seldom feel close to You when You are on my tongue?

How can I feel love for You in a noisy dining room, yet not feel anything when You are in me?

I guess that's how we're made.

Feelings are not important.

Intentions are.

My intentions are good, Lord. Make them better.

Let me love You, Lord, from now on, not in my usual tepid, phlegmatic, stupid way, but fervently, as the saints love You.

You have given me everything.

Your Son!

Your beautiful holy mother!

You made her my mother too!

Yourself!

You have even given me me.

What can I give You in return?

Nothing but me—and not all of me at that!

What a foul exchange!

Happy New Year, God.

*Dear God, Designer and Creator of this lovely world, your most welcome letter was waiting for me in the woods.*

I stumbled on it this morning—if one can stumble while sitting on a moss-covered rock.

Thanks, Lord. I love You too, in my own crazy way.

It took me a long time to realize the mail was in front of me; for I was full of the enthusiasm around me, the excitement of love and birth and the beginning of adventure among the wintergreen, the ferns, the strawberries and scores of plants I cannot name.

Every time I venture into Your woods I see another product of Your hands. Your creation has no limits.

I saw the letter at last; but it took me a long time to read it and a longer time to understand what I had read.

The snow had entirely disappeared. The first dandelions had come to dazzle us. The columbines had dared to send up their first shoots but were still too bashful to light their lanterns.

They need a little more encouragement from Your sun and shade and rain.

The violets are still hesitant and shy. They know it is May, but they haven't clearly heard Your word. They await Your full command.

We are impatient, God, we mortal men and women. We want everything in our gardens and our woods and fields to come up at once.

We do not realize that You have a time for each and every plant to bloom, to bear and to die. We want things to happen in our time, never in Yours.

I was looking at clover patches, trying to find one with four leaves. I was looking for little stones—shopping for gems for Your Mother's statue on my desk—and I was listening to the whisky voices of a dozen tipsy crows.

In spite of my absorption, I did see the birch and noticed it had crashed.

I was not surprised, exactly, for I had known it must someday fall. It was rotten at the core. It was majestic though and it towered high in Your blue sky, its white limbs writing poetry against the darkness of the surrounding trees.

It often made me remember George and his wife, and

thus it spoke to me of Your love.

"It was the biggest silver birch me and maw ever saw," George said, talking about a tree that must have been as beautiful as the fallen one.

"We pretty near said a prayer when we found it. We'd been cutting hemlock up to then; but all we got at the mill was seven dollars a thousand. We was mighty poor them days and cash was life to us.

"We was nigh desperate when we seen that tree. Big! Too big to put your arms around and pretty as the day itself.

"It took me and maw a day and a half to cut it down and some more time to trim the branches for the mill. Believe it or not, we got sixteen dollars for that one tree.

"And the money went to our heads. We took a boat to Barry's Bay and bought us a ride on the cars. Neither maw nor me ever rode the cars before. We was kind of excited, I tell you. The train ran up to Whitney them days. That's where we went. Fifty miles or more. Made it in one day!

"And we had us our second honeymoon!

"Maw and me was talking about it a minute or two before she died. It was sure nice to remember."

You turned a silver birch into a golden adventure for George and Maw, God, and into an imperishable memory.

How many ways You have of showing Your love to men!

Evidently a heavy gale had toppled this big birch, a fierce wind from the west; the bulk of it had fallen toward the east, toward the rising sun.

Part of the trunk stood up straight, like the monument that marks a grave. The rest of it lay across the rocks and the shrubbery of a clearing, part of it still attached to the broken stump.

The snows had covered it like a shroud during most of the winter. It had emerged now, a huddle and a scatter of beautiful dead white limbs, yet with budding leaves, making love to You, on what had been its topmost branches. The sap still ran through it!

You do not write in words, Lord.

You write in trees and flowers and grasses, in stones

and stars, in winds and waters, in men and women and in everything that can be seen or heard or smelled or touched or tasted.

It is never easy to put Your message into words.

Your letter had been tattooed on the upstanding part of the trunk, by the sharp hard beaks of many woodpeckers. It made a honeycomb pattern pleasant to the eye, a sort of secret cipher.

The burrowing crawling worms had added a cryptogram, with their many graceful s's.

(How the modern antique maker would love those worm tracks!)

The design puzzled me, but Love gave me the key.

Your Love for me, and mine for You.

So I understood and put it into words that others may read.

You share my letters to You. Why shouldn't I share Yours to me?

"I am the author of birth," You wrote. "You rejoice in the new life you see all about you, the evidence of My power and My love. It is good that you rejoice.

"Rejoice now because of this fallen tree. It is a true symbol of my Love. Through it I gave shade and shelter to birds and beasts and men.

"Through it I tempered the force of the wind and the heat of the sun for the tender plants beneath its branches.

"Through it I furnished young boys and girls with sheets of flimsy paper—a million colors blended in each square inch—that they might draw funny pictures on it or write messages to one another or fashion it into small canoes. (Were not the first canoes in this land made of this same birch bark?)

"Now I give you its wood for a hundred cheerful fires.

"In this tree I furnished fresh meat daily to the woodpeckers and strong sweet sap to the insects and the worms.

"Even the least and lowest of My creatures must have its daily bread; I must give it.

"You? So infinite is My love for you that I give you even Myself.

"My Body to eat! My Blood to drink!

"Should you not be strong and perfect and filled with joy? Should you not love Me more?

"Should you not feel close to Me, since I am so close to you?

"I am the author of birth.

"I am the author of death.

"How do you know there is not more joy in death than there is in birth?

"A woman when she has brought forth the child remembers her anguish no longer, for joy that a man has been born into the world.

"Yet, there is pain in every life and disappointment and frustration and terror, sometimes, even hideous despair—while only in death is the beginning of unending joy.

"A man is like a tree. I raise him from a tiny seed into a rival of the angels. I raise him high, if so it pleases Me. And I cut him down when I am ready.

"I use him for My own purposes: to give comfort and fruits and many other good things to My children, to show My love to the world, throughout the world. And to come to Me when I beckon.

"You I have given nearly eighty-five years. That is a long time, My son. You have not always stood straight in My wind and My sun and My sky. A long time ago you fell away from Me—even as the birch fell from its decaying trunk.

"Yet the sap still flows through this wreckage on the ground. The budding leaves have testified to this. My grace still lives in you.

"Pray that it continues to the end."

Lord, even in my most charitable inclinations toward myself, I have never thought of me as a birch tree, a symbol of purity.

I am a tough scrub bush, Lord.

My branches trail in the mire and the dust. They have been gnawed and scarred by many mean little sins, even as the limbs of small trees are nibbled and scratched by hares and rats and porcupines and other humble beasts.

I do not ask You to make me tall and splendid, though I know You could do it, even with such scrub-a-dub material as I am.

**134**     I do not ask to be a mighty oak or elm or maple, nor yet a fragrant pine or cedar.

Let me remain a squat, unaromatic, unnoticed, droopy bush. And let me stay rooted in the earth no longer than You plan.

Let Your grace seep into me, through the beautiful hands of Your Dear Lady, our Immaculate Mother. Let it expand, even though it bursts through my splintery, thorny bark and spills over into the earth around me.

Let it continue to circulate in me, even as the sap still works in this old tree on the ground!

Cut me down when You are ready, Lord, and take me to Your mill.

I will not bring You sixteen dollars, nor anything like that.

I hope only to fetch enough to provide for a honeymoon with You.

It will be exciting, Lord, to take my first ride on Your cars.

From here to heaven!

How long will it take?

Exciting, yes—and nice to remember all eternity.

Thanks again, God, for Your unexpected love letter.

Psalm 31

*It was a heavenly thrill to turn into the gate of my home after such a long absence and to see all the people I love.*

I know it will be even more heavenly when (and if) I turn into Your home and see all my loved ones there.

I was glad to see the river and the early flowers.

Did the Abominable Snowman dine on the clams all winter long? He littered the bed of the river with their shells. They stare up at a man through the clear chill waters, empty, lavender-lacquered, lovely; lying in pleasant disarray on the golden sands.

They present a poignant contrast to the first spring flowers. Their beauty is dead, but will endure for years; the living crocuses will perish in a night.

Yours is the only beauty that never dies.

Even now an unexpected snow flurry falls on them like a shroud.

The greatest thrill came to me in Arizona.

We were driving from Tucson toward Prescott and it was still light. We were high up in the mountains on a wide mesa.

It looked like the top of the world; I could see Your creation all around me. All around me and above me.

I liked the way You had sculptured the mountains in Tucson and the way You draped the sunset colors over them.

I liked the saguaro cacti that lifted their arms in prayer everywhere I could see.

The sun was sliding slowly down its western slope; and You were illuminating the white and gray clouds with red and gold.

The moon was high in the east, a strange full moon. The ghost of a moon. A blown dandelion of a moon. A moon a man could almost blow away with his breath, like so much gossamer.

The sun sank out of sight. I watched You mix Your oil colors.

I watched You smudge them gently with the charcoal powder You use to get Your night effects.

And I watched You set the sentinel stars.

(And I loved You, God, and admired You, and adored You, and thanked You for my life—with all the high points it has known, all the low points, all the sharp points, all the dull points, and all the points that were not points at all, but merely indications of Your love and care.)

Only for that moment did I love You intensely, God. But there have been few such moments in my life.

Perhaps I shall see that dandelion moon again. Perhaps not.

It does not matter really, but I shall see You, God—probably, at first, peeking from behind Your Mother's skirts and that is the thrill I live for.

What other thrill can compare with that?